8^10 *(Eight to the Tenth Power)*

8^10

(Eight to the

Tenth Power)

ALSO BY CHESTER ALFONSO

Dried Chicken Feet and Turtles with No Tongues

Featuring: *Dried Chicken Feet and Turtles with No Tongues; The Secretary and the Pain; and Back When.*

What Do They Say:

Featuring: *What Do They Say; Savenna, Yongse, and Danuri; and, Weimar and the Hotel Elephant.*

Negroes and the Half-White, Half-Black President:

Some strange words being said. Some mighty strange words.

8^10
(Eight to the Tenth Power)

A NOVEL BY

Chester Alfonso

CHESTER ALFONSO

FOR JUDY AND JACQUELINE

8^10 *(Eight to the Tenth Power)*

INTRODUCTION

I wish all of 8^10 *(Eight to the Tenth Power)* were fiction. Regrettably, some of it is true. Many may consider 8^10 *(Eight to the Tenth Power)* controversial: Controversial because it looks in a different sort of way at a sacrosanct and significant subject: A woman's right to abort.

It was a 1999 newspaper article that gained my interest. The article talked about the number of "legal" or "recorded" abortions that had occurred in the United States since the U.S. Supreme Court's January 22, 1973, Roe versus Wade decision: nearly fifty million. That's a lot. A whole bunch. According to a July 30, 2009 CNN report (CNN.COM Asia), China experiences more than 13 million abortions annually. Can you believe humans can kill – in one year – so many?

By the way: Eight to the tenth power equals: One billion, 73 million, 741 thousand, and eight hundred, twenty-four.

Take Care and be good.

Chester Alfonso

8^10 *(Eight to the Tenth Power)*

"By abortion, the mother does not learn to love, but kills even her own child to solve her problems. And by abortion, the father is told that he does not have to take any responsibility at all for the child he has brought into the world. That father is likely to put other women into the same trouble. So abortion just leads to more abortion. Any country that accepts abortion is not teaching the people to love, but to use any violence to get what they want. That is why the greatest destroyer of love and peace is abortion. "

- Mother Theresa

This quote comes from a speech delivered by Mother Teresa of Calcutta to the National Prayer Breakfast in Washington, DC on February 3, 1994.

8^10 *(Eight to the Tenth Power)*

1

Fifty/ maybe, 100/ 200/ maybe, even a billion.

Is there anybody counting?

Who cares? Who gives a damn?

2

Hiding in the raptures of her despair,

she hopes and waits on the latest of miracles.

Not knowing what to expect;

regretting the slightest touch,

even the ones that last, it seems only a few

seconds

before that time:

Before the procedure,

that will never be forgotten,

is scheduled to be performed.

But now her final decision,

and she is alone,

by herself.

And, the man that made her this way is

nowhere to be found.

3

8^10 *(Eight to the Tenth Power)*

In the Polish capital
of Warsaw,
Syvzaka Gorski rested his heavy arms on a small,
almost-clean table, in a tiny bistro,
on Aleje Jerozolimskie,
across from the Warszawa Centralna train station.
He would open, then shut, then open, then shut
his brown eyes that had
turned pink from too much worry
and his recent inability to sleep.
With his voice cracking, he ordered another drink – Vodka.
He was trying to drink away the thoughts
of Lyesya,
his sweet and lovely, 32-year-old daughter,
who was already a highly successful
manager at a major Polish telecommunication company.
She and her wonderful husband, Jakob,
had three beautiful children.
She had confided in Syvzaka:
telling him she was pregnant with another child.
Saying Jakob did not know.

CHESTER ALFONSO

Telling her farther she was afraid.
Said she had been cursed by a Warszawa gypsy:
a Roma sitting outside the Warszawa Centralna,
with her begging hands pushed
forward,
hoping her day of beseeching
would harvest a few zloty.
This Roma woman,
the one who usually dresses in a ragged,
ugly, green and red coat,
her head always wrapped in a greasy blue scarf,
had asked for money.
Lyesya responded by dropping a few groszy into the
detestable woman's cup.
Rather than being grateful,
the Roma woman
had shouted at Lyesya, demanded that she be given more.
Shocked and angry, Lyesya had refused.
That is when the old Roma,
with hateful words
and profanities coming from her mouth,

8^10 *(Eight to the Tenth Power)*

loudly predicted that she,

Lyesya,

would experience a personal tragedy:

Birth, to be followed by the child's total deformity,

and then the child's lingering and most painful death.

Lyesya told her father, Syvzaka, that she was terrified.

That it was not possible for her to have such a baby.

She had asked him to help her;

asking him to find a doctor

who would take care of her pregnancy.

That was why Syvzaka was sitting in this dreary bistro.

He was waiting the arrival of a man by the name of Jobal.

Jobal, he had been told, could easily, without any red tape,

make his daughter's pregnancy

and her future cursed-baby disappear.

And, for a fee that any common

but respectful Polish person could afford.

Looking through the smoke covered windows,

Syvzaka gestured to the waitress and asked for

still another Vodka.

He hoped Jobal would soon arrive, discuss his fee

and
describe how he, Jobal, could end his daughter's
dilemma.
The Vodka started to burn his gut.
Looking across the busy street,
he saw a huge man
getting out of an unwashed, dented,
black Mercedes.
The huge man was smoking a cigarette.
He looked tired, rumpled and angry.
Syvzaka prayed that the man was not Jobal.

4

And, the aborted, gotten-rid-of children
will have no chance to
see any sunrise or any sunset.
They will never jump with excitement
as horses run through pastures.
They will never
watch a baby play with any toy.
They will never tune-in to a
late night television show.

8^10 *(Eight to the Tenth Power)*

They will never notice any person
walking out of any crowded subway station.
And, never will they be bothered by
unpleasant, overbearing, in-a-hurry
bargain shoppers.
They will not be concerned with
income tax returns that must be corrected,
Sunday newspapers not being delivered,
or ice melting too quickly in a glass of lemonade.
And, they will have no worries about
not being on time for of an important lecture,
what words to use when writing a resume,
how to put a nosey mother-in-law in her place,
or eating too much of the wrong foods.
They will never wonder if they will
have enough money to pay the monthly rent.
Will not have to wonder how to dress up a lie to
make it sound truthful.
Will not have to wonder about learning
how to rollerblade skate,
or having to run on any morning

to catch any school bus.
For them, there will be no chance, ever, of
being proven right or wrong,
having to decide which persons to befriend,
pondering if they should take a weekend
flight to Jamaica.
They will never be afraid of loneliness,
of having a broken heart,
or acting silly.
They will never have an urge
to
visit a grandparent, an aunt or any high school
classmate.
There will be no encouragements to
go swimming
at a nearby swimming pool.
There will be no cravings for a Big Mac and fries.
They will never watch butterflies
seeking flowers to land on.
And, they will never know
the feeling of waking at four o'clock in the

8^10 *(Eight to the Tenth Power)*

morning after a terrible dream.
They'll never know which way is
north, south, east, west.
They will never realize what
petting a dog does to the soul
or how to make vegetable soup out
of homegrown vegetables.
And, they will never have a
chance to hear a church bell toll on any Sunday morning in
Padua, Italy,
Christchurch, New Zealand,
San Francisco, California, or Toronto, Canada.
Not a single one will ever hear a
presidential debate concerning
foreign and domestic policies.
Not a one will hear April rain falling
on rural Arkansas tin roofs
or lonely people laughing at anything
remotely amusing.
None of these will attend the
North Sea Jazz Festival

or the ones in Montreal and Montreux.
None of their feet will walk amongst protesters
protesting intolerable treatment of animals.
Not a single one of their voices will be allowed to
sing the national anthem of any country.

5

Somewhere out there,
where she did not know,
was the thing she kept trying
to get back.
The thing she had lost
long time ago: back fifteen-years-or-so
during a trip to Grand Rapids, up in Michigan
to visit her cousins, Nate and Wilma.
They were all fourteen, fifteen and sixteen.
Thought they knew everything life could teach.
Always, they were, running around the corner,
on Bryant Street,
pass the Do-Right Barber Shop,
where there were always
three or four chairs sitting out front

8^10 *(Eight to the Tenth Power)*

filled by older men who would always smile and say
funny and foolish things.
Then, returning, they would sit on the steps
of Aunt Kusi's big brick house;
the house left to her by Uncle Kildrew,
who'd died a few years ago.
They would sit there, on those steps,
telling tales, having fun, watching
people strolling by, nodding their heads.
People hurrying, they always seemed,
to someplace they should've been
long time ago or didn't want to be, at all.
Only two weeks, that's all the time she had,
then it was once again on the Greyhound Bus.
This time it would be heading south, back Down Home.
Back to the tenth grade
and math, civics, science, history and English classes.
Maybe, another chance of making
the varsity cheerleading squad.
Next summer, though, she would be back up here,
to Grand Rapids,

CHESTER ALFONSO

where everywhere there are paved streets
and brick houses with gas stoves.
When she arrived in Grand Rapids she was a virgin.
Had only kissed one boy in her entire life.
And, that was not really a serious kiss. Just a peck.
But, the boy from across that Grand Rapids' paved street,
the one who always walked pass the
Do-Right Barber Shop,
to the store, on Bryant Street,
with them, she knew he was the special one.
She could feel his specialness.
The first time he touched her hand
and held it for a little while – she
knew he was magic.
Knew by the way he said her name and smiled at her.
He told her things the stupid boys Down Home
never told her.
The first time he kissed her
he put his tongue right into her mouth.
Then he moved it round-and-round.
Her last two days in Grand Rapids were the best days she

8^10 *(Eight to the Tenth Power)*

had ever had in her life.
She couldn't do without him and his kissing,
his rubbing and his sweet and enticing up-north words.
Two times in those last two days
he laid her on his sister's made-up bed,
then he put his manly thing in her female thing
and made her cry real tears.
Made her smile with happiness, too.
On the Greyhound Bus,
traveling fast back to Decatur, in Alabama,
she dreamed about this boy.
He had promised to write her a letter every day.
Said he would never touch another girl as long as he lived.
She believed every word he had spoken.
Back home she knew her dreams, her hopes,
her love were real.
So, she continued to dream, hope, and love this boy.
But, after twenty long days
no letter from this boy reached her family's mailbox.
Her cousin, Wilma, did write, though.
Wilma said she and this boy,

CHESTER ALFONSO

the same boy the Decatur, Alabama girl loved,
had gone to a high school dance together.
But, she wrote, nothing had happened between them
other than a short kiss
and a little playing around.
Nothing serious, she claimed.
So, this Decatur, Alabama girl,
a few months before turning fifteen,
started thinking that the boy from Grand Rapids
might have lied about writing her and loving her.
Thinking, maybe, he had not meant all he had promised
about always being faithful, and so on.
She started paying more attention to her studies and
practicing harder to become a varsity cheerleader.
Then, she found out she was in real trouble:
she missed her period. Then she missed another one.
Couldn't sleep too well. So afraid.
Knowing she may have crossed into a scary swamp
where her soul would be muddied and
mosquitoes would be forever stinging her memories.
Confused and frightened, she didn't know what to do.

8^10 *(Eight to the Tenth Power)*

How could she explain the love, the craving,
the joy, the passion she had for this Grand Rapids boy?
Momma and daddy and grandma and grandpa
were too old and too set in their ways to understand.
Everyday before school, during each class,
on the way from school, at night, all the time she prayed
for God's help.
Soon, momma and daddy, but not grandma and grandpa,
became aware.
Then, on a cloudy Monday morning,
they made her get in the back seat of
their new Chevy Impala.
Then, they drove her over a hundred miles
to Nashville, in Tennessee.
That's where that special doctor;
a man with a big, round face and
yellow hair, went through her private parts,
into her belly and removed what life that boy
up in Grand Rapids had given her.

6

And, what about the unborn

CHESTER ALFONSO

who face the Abortion Executioners?
For them there will be
no Halloween nights of tricks or treats.
They will have no quiet days sitting on river banks
throwing terrified fish back
into warm salt water.
They will have no glorious
moments signing autographs.
For them there will be no long drives
in twenty-wheelers across the Rockies,
no sunning on any beach in the Caribbean.
And, they will never
change a diaper or put powder on a baby's
cleaned behind.
They will not cut grocery coupons
from weekend newspapers,
play Tic-Tac-Toe against any sibling,
lay in bed with a terrible head cold,
or cry at a love one's funeral.
Because of the Abortion Executioners,
they'll never have a chance to

8^10 *(Eight to the Tenth Power)*

sing a lullaby, a hymn;

send or receive flowers,

pour milk onto morning cereal,

open a checking account,

or say a silent prayer.

Imagine being deprived forever of

wanting to run faster than the fastest runner.

Imagine being deprived of having a fifth grade

class in art appreciation,

geography, science, or mathematics,

of washing after-dinner dishes,

or riding on any of Euro Disney's roller coasters.

Imagine never having the opportunity to

dream about discovering a cure for cancer,

sickle cell, heart disease, diabetes,

Alzheimer's, influenza, the common cold,

HIV/AIDS, autism or cerebral palsy.

Because of the Abortion Executioners,

these unfortunate ones will be stripped

of all chances to become destitute,

beggar, wealthy, a high school principle,

or the manager of some super market.
And, they will be stripped of ever
stroking a shy kitten or owning a tricycle.
They will be stripped of possessing
one single fantasy,
or an unwarranted doubt.
Nor will they be allowed to
hope for the demise of the neighborhood bully
or for steamy summer days to end.
They will not feel front teeth starting to grow
or have a best friend stop by for some juicy gossip.
Because of the Abortion Executioners,
these misfortunate ones will be
forever robbed of the right to
wake up in the morning, get out of bed, and sigh;
to tell someone they are beautiful,
play a game of pool,
or think about what might happen next week.

7

Nobody knew.

Not a soul came close.

8^10 *(Eight to the Tenth Power)*

The release of the schoolgirl's screams
traveled through the atmosphere
before settling on some unconcerned nerve.
An unconcerned nerve
too troubled with its own problems
to pay attention to any schoolgirl's scream
coming from that place
schoolgirls go when schoolgirls
want to end the life schoolgirls are carrying
but not wanting.

8

None will ever be worried about
the Law School Admission Test
or being scratched from any team's starting lineup.
None will have a chance of playing
blackjack at Caesars Palace.
None will ever participate in a teachers' strike.
None will ever light a candle.
For them there will be no anger, not ever, about
being demoted for an invalid reason.
They will show no anger because someone yelled

in their faces.

They will never be concerned over being lied

about by distant relatives.

Never will they care that a loan was denied

because of gender, race, religion, or age.

There will be no chance of ever seeing

a ballerina perform at Lincoln Center,

chickens being led to slaughter,

blues singers moaning their blues

at blues joints,

or a drunk staggering down a crowed London street.

They will be denied the opportunity to ever

drive too far down the wrong country road,

walk across a dried river bed,

watch the Minneapolis New Year's fireworks show,

or order a Chinese meal

at a restaurant in Maracay.

9

In the sterile surroundings,

while waiting for the

lady in the light-blue uniform to return

8^10 *(Eight to the Tenth Power)*

with the papers that were signed two weeks ago,

the papers stipulating what

procedures will take place,

she reads an article from the pages of

Southern Living

explaining how to make great apple pies.

10

Those prematurely taken in pieces

from the womb

will never

put earphones to their ears to listen to any music,

become a fugitive from justice,

write a book about anything,

or embellish a story about anyone.

They will not be available to accomplish something

simple, like:

folding a handkerchief, slicing a tomato,

putting coins in a parking meter,

shining a pair of shoes the night before going

on a job interview,

or turning the pages of a calendar

from one month to the next.
They will never be around for
a mother's tale about how busy her work day was.
They won't be around to inquiry about a sister,
brother, or a cousin.
Will not be around to receive a pat on the back for
doing something well.
Won't be around for the times when things
important were forgotten
and things not important were remembered.
They will be barred forever from tasting
salt, pepper, onions or pineapple.
Barred from hearing the sound of an oncoming
Harley Davidson motorcycle or
the sweetness of a tenor saxophone
being blown on a night club's stage.
Nor will they ever have a chance to excel,
even at hop-scotch.

11

Some data collector says worldwide
there might be forty-five million a year.

8^10 *(Eight to the Tenth Power)*

That's four hundred and fifty million in ten years.
Since Roe versus Wade, January 1973,
some forty years ago;
at a rate of 45 million a year,
the number comes to one billion, eight hundred million.
Has war, famine, genocide, disease
killed so many?
Has ignorance, religion, or politics
killed so many?
Was Number forty-five million
a boy or a girl?
What about Number 1 million?
was it a He or a She,
a Jew, Christian, Hindu, Muslim, or Buddhist,
or a nonbeliever?
Was Number 99 thousand and fifteen a redhead?
Was Number 359
a boy or a girl?
Was that boy or girl gonna grow up
in Brazil, Turkey,

the Czech Republic, Honduras, Laos?
Was that boy or girl gonna have
happy times or miserable times?
Was that boy or girl gonna live
two blocks from your door or in a nearby town?
Number ten?
What sex was number ten?
Was Number five gonna write with the
left-hand or right-hand?

12

<u>Pause</u>

The farmer planted his seeds into the soil.
He, then, carefully nourished the seeds.
At night, he and wife, prayed for rain.
But, the rain never did come.
All the planting, seeding, nourishing
and never a crop.
Year after year, the same farmer,
with the same wife, carefully planted his seeds.
Afterwards, he and his wife did all the right things
to ensure the crop's growth.

8^10 *(Eight to the Tenth Power)*

The two of them,
with the help of neighbors and their pastor -
prayed for rain, just a few drops.
But, no rain came and, again, no crop.
Then, after years of disappointment,
their prayers were finally answered.
The rains came.
Unknown to everyone but the farmer and his wife
the fields started to show some life.
Suddenly, the wife realized how much work
she would have to do once the crops
began to bloom.
She knew she would no longer be able to enjoy her
Wednesdays and Fridays playing bridge
with her three best friends.
Her husband and she would be too busy tending the
fields and harvesting the crop.
Late one night, before the sprouts began to show,
she told her husband how much she feared losing
her freedom; how much work they would
eventually be engaged in.

CHESTER ALFONSO

She told him she no longer wanted to grow the crop.
The farmer, deeply in love with his wife, agreed to
do whatever necessary to assure
her happiness and their togetherness.
So, after two more discussions, they finally agreed:
They would, late at night, when no one could see
them, go into the field and spread chemicals that
would destroy the budding crops.
Two day later, working from mid-night
until 4am, they sprayed the chemicals
over the budding crops.
All of a sudden, what they had prayed for
was gone, ruined, wiped out, destroyed.
The farmer and his wife,
decided to never pray for any more rain.
They said they were tired of praying;
tired of being disappointed.
They vowed to never again ask the pastor to render
a prayer concerning anything on their behalf
They no longer wanted to be farmers.
While resting and recovering from their

8^10 *(Eight to the Tenth Power)*

destructive deed, they decided they would go on

vacation to Ireland, Scotland, and Poland.

13

Pause

Malabo, a place where most, for entertainment,

have only a small radio and

something as simple as an occasional

and decent *char siu bao bun*.

The common folks of Malabo

have always been as poor as their commonness.

The lazy ones tarry

around falling and failing shacks.

The ones not so lazy

clean the floors, shine the cars,

and make the beds of the rich.

The criminal ones' ascribed behavior

is to steal from the not so lazy ones,

while watching the wealthy men,

sitting in their chauffeured-driven,

air conditioned automobiles,

drink their cooled, imported

CHESTER ALFONSO

        bottled water,
        as their women
sashay down *Plaza De La Independencia* and
     the few other paved avenues,
  wearing on their wrists Patek Phillipe,
  with Yves Saint Laurent, Chanel, Versace
       covering their thin,
    delicious-to-look-at bodies.
   Bodies nourished at evening dinners,
 away from their recently purchased palaces,
      at the overly expensive
Sofitel Malabo President Palace's El Basile,
where their leftovers are always boxed and
placed into their latest Hermes Birkin bag.
   They, the delicious-to-look-at wives
      or the "kept-women,"
speak their broken French, English, or Spanish,
     no matter how they try not to,
with a Fang, Bube, or Annobonese accent.
Pretty girls, born, raised and recently removed
      by the rich oil-men from

8^10 *(Eight to the Tenth Power)*

their Equatorial Guinea squalor.
Rich men, with their delicious-to-look-at
wives or their "kept-women,"
always living in their well-guarded mansions.
These men, these unrighteous scoundrels –
are the ones with the
most Central African francs and the
least amount of human scruples.
And, they, too, are the ones with the fewest children;
never more than two.
One – if not both – must be a boy.
It is whispered, though,
that these scoundrel-men have the
most diverse and devastating sex
of any men in Equatorial Guinea.
It is also told, but always in hushed tones,
that these scoundrel-men perform ungodly
and evil sexual acts
with their "bought-off-the-beaches-of-Rio Muni" wives
and their "kept-women."
The whispering queens, the gossiping maidens –

called, maids,
tell stories of bloodied sheets and
spoiled ladies' underwear awashed in dirty blood.
They tell stories of medical operations
performed by European doctors
from Paris, Lyon, Lisbon;
even an occasional operation performed by a
certain witch doctor from that place called
Douala, in Cameroon.
Saying these rich descendents of the Devil will allow
their bought-wives to produce only two children.
They are forbidden from having
more, regardless the number of times
they become pregnant.
And, so, because of the gossiping maids,
everybody knows why there is so much blood,
and why after the blood, the delicious-to-look-at
ladies are not seen for weeks walking along
Plaza De La Independencia wearing their Yves Saint
Laurent, their Chanel, their Versace.

14

8^10 *(Eight to the Tenth Power)*

These lives, with all future and hope erased,

will never be touched by rain drops,

sentiment or sadness.

They will have no last minute

arrangements go awry.

Nor will they ever cause any person to be

disappointed.

Not once will they wonder what makes

the world go round.

They, with all future and hope erased,

will never know a

right foot from a left foot,

sadness from happiness,

joy from gloom, healing from hurting.

And, they will never imagine what makes anything

wonderful or wretched.

Alas: They will die before they are ever borne.

They will sleep with no chance of ever being

awakened.

Their eyes will never open, never see.

Never will they appreciate the

beauty of a sincere smile.
They will not notice a bird in search of a worm,
or a raccoon climbing a tree.
They will not appreciate any painting
hanging in any
museum.
Sadly,
they will be deprived forever of
the simplest gesture.
Will be deprived of experiencing
a most wonderful evening sitting alone
and drinking a cooled glass of water.
Will be deprived of ever seeing
the bright faces of a young couple in love.
Not once will they have any dreams of visiting
India, the Bahamas, Bucharest, Singapore,
Antananarivo, Tampa, Cape Town, Dusseldorf,
Santa Maria, Helsinki, or Charlottesville.
They will not cross into a neighbor's backyard to
enjoy barbequed chicken.
Not once will they drive out to

8^10 *(Eight to the Tenth Power)*

the car dealerships on the outskirts
of Salt Lake City or Russellville, or Danville.
Because they are butchered,
they are forever removed from shame, anger,
prejudice, fear.
Because of the unforgiving butchers,
they will never feel weak, strong, envy,
mediocre.
Due to the abortion slicers-and dicers,
they will never taste a soft drink,
red wine, whisky, lemon juice, apple cider.
Neither will they enter any shoe store in
Boulder, Seoul, Stockholm, Rome,
or Santa Ana de los Cuatro Ríos de Cuenca.

15

<u>Pause</u>

What would the teachers and the professors
of mathematics, architecture, drama,
literature, history, engineering,
philosophy, art, medicine, law, anthropology, economics,
physics, language, geography, biology, computer science,

chemistry, music, and psychology
teach
if someone, cavalierly,
or even with subsequent regret and
remorse –
had, because they believed in "Choice,"
stopped the breathing of an unborn,
let us say:
Verdi, Raphael, Pasteur, Lincoln, Kant,
Euripides, Botticelli, Gauguin, Einstein,
Brahms, Hugo, Gershwin, Curie, Disney,
Chopin, Schuman, Marx, Michelangelo, Mao,
Cervantes, Hesse, Shostakovich, Van Rijn,
Rachmaninoff, Pascal, Newton, Morrison,
Dostoyevsky, Homer, Archimedes, Galileo, Camus,
Dante, Mother Teresa, Cezanne, da Vinci,
Mahler, Socrates, Hughes, Bontemps, Ovid,
William Blake, St. Paul, Shakespeare, Braille, Reuben,
Hayden, Mendeleev, Whitney, Edison, Darwin,
Lenin, Picasso, Caesar, Eliot, Baldwin, Yeats, Chekov,
Wright, Amis, Dylan, Ellington, Kipling, Bacon, Cezanne,

8^10 *(Eight to the Tenth Power)*

Diego Velasquez, Byron, Nasser, Goya, O'Keefe,
Chaucer, Stendhal, Watt, Niepce, Sikorsky, Herschel,
Matisse, Wyatt, M.L. King, Shiva, Monet,
Virginia Woolf, Menninger, Bettelheim, Renoir,
Franz Kafka, Bernstein, Satchmo, Twain, Volta,
Joseph Turner, Chagall, Poussin, Holbein, Bose,
Handel, Ho Chi Minh, Jung, Cleopatra,
Chekhov, Franklin, Gibran, Zola, Bach,
Ezra Pound, Liszt, Tchaikovsky, Vivaldi,
Nijinsky, Horowitz, Grand Master Flash,
Monk, Steve Jobs, and, or Pasteur?

16

To save the mothers' lives, they tell us,
the new lives must be decimated.
The new lives , they tell us,
must be removed, finished, killed.
To save the mothers' lives, they tell us,
the new lives must be annihilated.
And, because the new lives are killed,
the liberated mothers will never
worry themselves about not relaxing after

CHESTER ALFONSO

tiring days of assembling sprockets
on some assembly line.
Because they are annihilated,
the freed mothers will never have to
contemplate not taking
long walks or engaging in long
sessions at fitness centers,
hoping to shed nine or ten pounds.
Because the mothers' lives must be saved,
the future lives of children must be
disposed of, sacrificed.
The future children, having been disposed of,
will not have the ability to
ever give thought to lines and colors on any canvas
drawn by any artist that was recently read about -
who was rumored to have been born with no sight,
but, thanks to God, was born.
Because the future children must be
sacrificed for the sake
of the mothers' lives,
they, the future children, will be eternally robbed

8^10 *(Eight to the Tenth Power)*

of the chance to ever buy a comic book,
the chance to try and sooth a suddenly arrived
headache that is attempting to
disrupt a pleasant afternoon
watching youngsters fly kites in the
field next to the big lake
on the east side of the city.
And, these potential school children
will never know a parent.
Removed, they will be, of
ever witnessing a terrified squirrel
frozen in a road by oncoming traffic,
hearing screams of other squirrels,
who are frightened, worried that their terrified
friend will be killed,
then left on that road for ugly vultures to peck away
its fur and bone.
Not once will these aborted children
get a splinter in a finger,
stump a toe, or scar a knee.
Not once will they be playfully slapped

upside the head by a pal.
Nor will they ever dial a wrong telephone number.

17

Guess what, girl?
The other day,
these smart-looking, smart-acting bitches came to
the school. To Miss Lemon's health class.
The class where there ain't nothing but girls.
Said they was gonna explain what abortions
be all 'bout.
Right from the git-go,
I knowed them to be some out-right lying hoes.
One was white. One was black.
The other one looking like she be Mexican or Rican.
They stood right
'fo us, acting like they know more'n what we do.
They started telling how, up in New York City
if a thousand black women,
'specially our age black women,
git
knocked-up, mor'n half of 'em

8^10 *(Eight to the Tenth Power)*

end up gittin'
rid of the damn thang.
Them hos claimed
that almost six outta ten black women
up in New York City
end up gittin' a 'bortion.
Said, that goes to show, if they doin' it up north, in
New York, in the Big Apple, then,
'bortions can't be all that bad.
They said them 'bortions, be alright if you be
knowin' from the git-go that you ain't got 'nough
money and time to take care of a baby.
Put it in our heads that gittin' rid
of some damn, soon-to be black crumbsnatcher is
sortta like gittin' rid
of anything you don't want that's gonna
hold you down, hold you back, make you suffer.
They said, 'pending on your condition,
like how you doin' in school,
what kind'a family you be comin' from,
and what kind'a plans you got after graduatin',

CHESTER ALFONSO

if you graduate,
they said 'bortions probably
the best thing for us black women, living in areas
where we be livin'.
Told us we all got a choice, though.
This Rican or Mexican or Cuban –
whatever the hell she is,
said we had to do what's right by us.
Don't listen to nobody else but our ownself.
Can you 'blieve that shit?
Like I said,
them bitches was straight-out bold.
Like they be
saying it ain't too bad a thang
for us blacks and browns to
be gittin' the knife
but they ain't said shit 'bout
them white bitches gittin' pregnant
by these trifling, black-ass,
wanna-be players, po motherfuckers.
And, we all knows what them white

8^10 *(Eight to the Tenth Power)*

skanks go and do.
Yea, girl, you know it: Fo you can turn 'round
them white, wanta-be-sistas,
done gone and got
rid of them half-breeds they be carrying.
Naw, these three bitches gone and
brought their high-class,
thanking-they-educated asses where we be.
I just looked at 'em. Said to myself:
"Ain't nobody gonna tell me
what to do wit my pussy.
If I get knocked up, so fuckin' what?"
One thang I know, though, they
didn't built that Planned Parenthood Center,
over on Massey Street,
right here in our neighborhood, for nothing.
They built that place so we can have
somewhere to take our black asses so we can keep
outta having a bunch of
crying, begging, ghetto-ass, welfare babies.
So, I just looked at them bitches.

CHESTER ALFONSO

Janelsola, that kinda fat girl,
who LaBurk be fuckin',
she said she didn't
b'lieve black women
be having that many 'bortions.
Said she don't b'lieve nobody,
no matter what they color be,
gonna up and kill that many babies.
Them three bitches
looked at her like she be crazy.
Told her black women
was probably having more'n
what the real records show.
But you know what? I ain't gonna stop doin' what I
be always doin'.
Hell, Viscount, that crazy-ass mo-fo,
sex machine of mine,
would leave my ass if I told him we
had to slowdown screwing just
'cause I be 'fraid of gittin' big.
He'll drop my ass in a half-minute.

8^10 *(Eight to the Tenth Power)*

*Girl, you and I both know
there be a whole bunch'a
bitches out here willin' to screw Viscount
til they pass-out.
And, I ain't 'bout to tell Viscount to start using
some damn rubber, either.
That fool don't know what that is.
So, if I ever get knocked-up,
I'm'a take my ass over to that
clinic on Massey Street
and let them folks take care of it.
Shit, that's how come they builded that thang so
close to us.*

18

The aborted ones will never know
what makes people smile, what makes them laugh,
makes them cry,
makes them complain about things that will
eventually be alright.
The aborted ones will never offer a comment
concerning people who constantly criticize,

                lie, get drunk, never bathe, eat too much.
                  Nor will they close their eyes and
                        fall into a deep sleep
in a bed made earlier in the day by someone other
                            than themselves.
They will not possess the things the living take for
                              granted, like:
              going across town to talk to a friend
            about next week's field trip to Brisbane
        and whether there will be time to run up and
                          down the Gold Coast.
Not once will the aborted ones be able to eat
                    a peanut butter sandwich,
               enjoy October Fest in Munich,
                drink tea in a Charleston cafe,
or eat fish cakes at Dublin's *Brazen Head*.
               They will never know the discomfort
           of sitting next to a snoring passenger on a
             fully booked, seventeen-hour flight,
or that someone in China, Peru, Mali, Tasmania will
                            soon be mourned.

8^10 *(Eight to the Tenth Power)*

How sad it must be to never get a chance to hear
recordings of Louis Armstrong, Johnny Cash
Ella, Wilson Pickett, Loretta Lynn,
Muddy Waters, Merle Haggard, Ravel, Beethoven;
or the sound of a rushing tide,
the muted roar of a small lion calling for its mother,
or the words of a crazed poet reciting his poems
in a remote corner of Hyde Park.
Removed, they will be, from ever
dozing in a big chair, in a small room;
participating in a spelling bee,
a talent show or a cook-off.
Removed, they are, from buying
something unusual at a flea market,
or watching a television game show
where nobody ever wins.

19

They had all gathered, formally attired, important minds.
Smiles. Pats on the backs.
Champaign glasses were raised
to acknowledge a slim, high-browed woman,

who walked alone,
wearing a flowing silk dress with
diamonds up and down the sleeves.
Everyone roses, applauded.
Many more smiles and nodding of the heads.
Gracefully, she walked onto the stage.
A podium slowly rose,
upon which she laid a single sheet of paper
containing well rehearsed words.
The higher echelon knew what she might say,
who would be honored,
who might be praised, who would receive
the much regarded and most prestigious award.
Gesturing with her small hands,
she told them to be seated,
to finish eating
their well prepared food.
Told them this would be a great evening,
lots of fun among
special and wonderful friends.
The minister, 56-years-old, with a doctorial degree in

8^10 *(Eight to the Tenth Power)*

divinity, laughed aloud,

but not his companion, a woman, twenty-four,

with no degree, diploma, or certificate in anything.

Near the front, at a table occupied by the likable

U.S. senator from New York,

a joke was being told by the senator's wife, Helen,

about a black, female waiter who slipped on a

slice of bacon, lost her balance,

fell to the floor but never spilled a drop of the expensive

wine she was carrying, even though she, this waiter,

in falling, had broken her arm.

The senator, embarrassed, smiled and said:

"Helen, what's the punch line?"

Helen, replied:

"Better hope you don't slip on a slice of bacon.

But, if you do, you better hope its been fried."

The dark-skinned waiters and waitresses,

professionals at pouring water, bringing meals,

removing plates, and refilling wine glasses,

pretended they had not heard

the senator's wife crude words.

CHESTER ALFONSO

They continued their work;
invisible to the highly educated,
very liberal attendees.
There were Raven, Juanita, Jonathan,
Brooke, LeVan, Tony, Dalia, Adam, and TraJuan.
They were the best at what they did, which
included being silent and invisible.
The slim, high-browed woman wearing the flowing silk
dress, with expensive diamonds up and down the sleeves,
returned to the stage and began to
introduce the keynote speaker. A person, she said,
with the highest sense of giving and
loving for all mankind.
Said, no one had given more to society
than this great humanitarian.
Told the gathered elite and prosperous humanitarians
about the individual's
accomplishments and achievements.
Said, she was honored to be on the same planet as this
great person.
Then, she called the name of the

8^10 *(Eight to the Tenth Power)*

U.S. Congresswoman from Maine.

The congresswoman from Maine,

after forty seconds of applause,

spoke for ten minutes and thirty seconds, eyes all teary.

She mentioned Margaret's name five times.

Said how proud she was to have

received the previous year's award.

How Margaret's words had changed all their lives;

made them keenly aware and more appreciative

of their role in shaping humanity.

Then she was joined on stage,

again, by the slim, high browed woman.

Together they announced the new winner of the award:

"The Planned Parenthood Federation of America

Margaret Sanger Award."

The minister, fifty-six, with a doctorial degree in divinity,

stood to the shouts, applause, and the touching of his

shoulders, arms and hands.

His black face was

hard and confident from the years of diligently preaching

in the poorest regions of the Deep South:

CHESTER ALFONSO

Mississippi, Louisiana, Alabama, and Georgia.
To be given this award! Lord!
This was more than he had ever
hoped for. Ever dreamed of.
He knew right then,
even before his feet reached the stage,
that he would do everything he could to make
the Planned Parenthood organization proud.
When he began his speech,
he spoke, not as he had spoken
a few days earlier before a
multitude of Southern Baptists at the Holy Redeemer
Baptist Church that had been filled with poor,
uneducated, obese, too-many-children black folks.
No, tonight, before this almost lily-white crowd,
with his high-yellow,
sorta-skinny, twenty-four-year-old,
sitting and twisting in her seat,
he spoke, not like some refugee from his birth place,
Choctaw County, Mississippi,
but like the holder of a PhD

8^10 *(Eight to the Tenth Power)*

from the Yale School of Divinity.
Not once did he extract from his coat pocket
the neatly folded, white
handkerchief to wipe sweat from his black face.
Not once did he speak in a fashion his
24-year-old sweet-thing could recognize.
The preacher man told how he had been awakened
in the middle of the night
from a dream too real to really be a dream.
A dream about the overflowing numbers of poor, ignorant,
starving, homeless, destitute, violent, unemployed and
unemployable grown-folks and children
climbing over the walls that separate them from the
educated, the rich, the
healthy, the beautiful, the wise,
and mostly white communities.
Vividly, he saw
the masses of scum flooding the grounds,
the homes, the schools, the restaurants,
and the churches of the elite.
Of the better-class.

Of the blessed multitude.

Of the fortunate society.

Said he woke up covered in sweat.

He was shaking, frightened.

Being moved by God's Spirit.

At that moment he knew something rightful,

something righteous was upon him.

The very next day God revealed to him what that

righteousness was about to do.

Seemingly, out of nowhere,

he was contacted by

the Planned Parenthood organization.

They requested that he lend his powerful voice,

educated mind, unique talents,

and immense influence among black people and the poor,

they had said,

in the construction and placement of hundreds of new,

state-of-the-art

Planned Parenthood Reproductive Clinics.

These new facilities, they explained,

were to be built, for the most part,

8^10 *(Eight to the Tenth Power)*

in the black and brown neighborhoods of America.
For, it is in the black and brown neighborhoods,
they told him, where the poorest,
least educated, all-the-time-pregnant,
all-the-time-in-poverty,
all-the-time-engaged-in-criminal-activity people live.
Because of his dream, he knew he had
no choice but to help
the good folks at Planned Parenthood.
He told the mesmerized crowd that
he had long admired the greatness
of Margaret Sanger and her Planned Parenthood
organization.
He said there were not many men or women her equal.
Said he held her in higher regard
than he did the great politicians,
the renowned academics,
the most creative scientists,
the most gifted lawyers,
sport heroes, or the best entertainers.
He spoke about the great things Margaret Sanger

and Planned Parenthood had done,
especially, in the African American and Latino
communities.
Communities filled with dilapidated morals,
dilapidated minds, and dilapidated homes.
Planned Parenthood, he said, wanted to assist
those whose future dictated a life surrounded by
abundant filth, ostentatious poverty,
and too many grotesquely conceived babies.
His speech had hit its stride.
The words were easily flowing.
He told them that
because of the teachings of Margaret Sanger,
the Planned Parenthood organization,
and their reproductive clinics,
he was able to see a
discernible difference
in the birth rates of these catastrophic women;
too many of them still in high school,
some, even in middle school.
As the preacher man reached for a glass of water,

8^10 *(Eight to the Tenth Power)*

his mind wandered, ever so slightly:

He thought about "Her,"

the 24-year-old beautiful "Thing" sitting at his table.

Already, the Planned Parenthood clinics had taken

two babies from her belly, yet, her body was still

magnificent, ravishing, and capable of great performances.

She was nothing more than a whore, he thought,

who loved to love him.

She had told him that abortion, including

her own, were wrong.

Had said she had read somewhere that Margaret Sanger

had been a racist, had adored Hitler,

hated black people, hated poor people

and the children they produced,

but loved the Klan.

Preacher man, with the Yale PhD, had to remind her

that this award,

the one he was receiving,

had been presented to one of her heroes:

Doctor, Reverend Martin Luther King, Junior.

He reminded her that many who had fought racism,

great champions of human rights, had also
accepted this most prized award.
Told her names she, being a low-rung, high-yellow,
black whore, did not know,
such as:
Katharine Hepburn, Justice Harry Blackmun,
Madam Sadat,
John D. Rockefeller III; Mary Calderone,
and his favorite
that is,
other than Doctor King:
Hillary Rodham Clinton.
Simply by agreeing to persuade ignorant, poor,
scumbag, ghetto dwellers
to allow for more control over
their procreation processes,
he was being honored, praised,
lifted to new heights of dignity.
He was a Doctor of Divinity, he knew his religions
as well as anyone,
better than ninety-nine percent of the people.

8^10 *(Eight to the Tenth Power)*

He knew what the Bible said

and he knew its interpretations.

Therefore, regardless of his actions, as a Christian man,

he always knew he would be forgiven.

He all the time recited the words he holds

so close to his heart:

"Then Peter came to Jesus and asked,

'Lord, how many times shall I forgive my brother

when he sins against me?

Up to seven times?'

Jesus answered,

'I tell you, not seven times, but seventy-seven times'."

20

Some are smothered, others mutilated,

some have been bludgeoned,

before telling anyone how they felt,

before typing or writing a single word,

or before brushing teeth before bedtime.

Others are quashed, nullified, purged.

Some have been pulverized,

while in the womb anticipating a long life

where maybe they could see slow autumns
beautifying the landscapes of New England,
with hanging clouds enveloping Bar Harbor, Maine.
Others are quenched, destroyed, slain,
undone before
ever having a chance to cross
the International Date Line,
before attempting to solve a complicated algebra
problem,
or before peeling potatoes and shucking corn for a
Thanksgiving dinner.
Some are extirpated, mangled, invalidated, erased
before
knowing the fastest route from Timbuktu to Goa,
before caring what someone will say about a newly
purchased coat, or before walking down
Ave des Champs-Elysées.
Others are canceled-out, eliminated, butchered,
pulverized prior to a first birthday,
before having a chance to pee into a diaper,
prior to falling from a pair of roller skates,

8^10 *(Eight to the Tenth Power)*

or prior to eating a cookie
while a mommy and a daddy are
talking about the latest news.
Some are executed, destructed, suffocated,
massacred before they
can breathe one day of life,
before playing, just once, with a
Chucky Cheese clown,
or before learning to be quiet when its nap time in
a kindergarten classroom.

21

Her name:
Isadora Catalina de la Balc.
She's a mestizo, from
Santiago's Vitacura neighborhood.
Most believed God had never made a more lovely,
sophisticated,
dignified, exquisite, pleasant, and alluring woman,
as the magnificent, Isadora Catalina de la Balc.
Isadora, with the genetically inherited gifted mind;
a law student at the

CHESTER ALFONSO

Pontificia Universidad Católica de Chile.
It had been twenty-three years since her birth
in one of the most aristocratic
sectors of Santiago.
But, on this day,
the beautiful Isadora Catalina de la Balc gazed
across the desk at a serious looking woman,
and said:
"Tell me in precise language what this will entail."
The woman, pausing, frowning, hoping this was not a trick,
replied:
"We, no, I, will make absolutely certain
that you are within the timeframe that will allow this to
safely take place.
Then you will go, on a certain day, between 9am and 10am,
to a specific hotel, with a designated room number.
At this location you will wait until
you receive additional instructions.
These instructions will be provided by one of my aides.
This aide will come to you using
words that only you will recognize.

8^10 *(Eight to the Tenth Power)*

At that time you, with the assistance of my aide,
will start your preparations.
You will be given directions and assistance
on how to prepare."
Isadora Catalina de la Balc did not flinch, she just smiled:
"How soon will I be able to return to my studies?"
"The procedure will take place at the start of
the student holiday period.
You will have a two week break; more than enough time to
recover.
When you return to your studies,
you will be as good as new, but
you must not have vaginal sex
for at least six weeks afterwards."
She paused, then continued:
"But, above all, you must not tell a single soul.
As a future lawyer, you know, for sure, that in Chile,
this – the abortion – is forbidden - is illegal.
It is so, even for someone of your pedigree,
wealth, and power."
Isadora Catalina de la Balc flicking a small fly

from her part-European shoulder,
considered the serious woman and said:
"I want to know how you will perform this procedure.
I want to be assured that everything will be removed.
I want to feel safe and I don't want any scars left anywhere
on my body.
Nor do I want a single cell
of this bastard to remain in my body.
You see, in July,
I will be off to Cannes and the French Rivera.
Can you imagine me walking along
a beach with a scarred body?"
The physician assistant's lips parted,
her cheeks hardened, she felt warm:
"Have you heard of the suction curettage method?
What about the vacuum aspiration method?
With the vacuum aspiration,
some refer to it as the suction curettage method,
the fetus, your baby, will be sucked out of you.
If the fetus, or if you prefer, the baby,
is not entirely sucked-out, I'll still be able to

8^10 *(Eight to the Tenth Power)*

remove the remaining bits and pieces. All of them.

I will make sure not a trace is left in your body.

As for scars, I can assure you there will be no scars.

No man, or woman, for that matter,

will ever detect what has happened.

No one will ever know, other that you, my aide,

and I, that you have had an abortion"

Having received such assurance,

Isadora Catalina de la Balc rose

and without the slightest display of emotions, said:

"Make contact within five days;

not later than the start of the next month

I want to be rid of this pathetic

inconvenience as quickly as possible.

I want you to permanently remove it from my body

and my mind.

And, I want it done as soon as it can be done.

Do you understand?"

With her sensuous and inviting hips swaying,

Isadora Catalina de la Balc walked away.

22

CHESTER ALFONSO

Because they are done away with,
not a single one will ever know
what day follows Wednesday,
when snow usually starts melting on Mount Kenya,
or why Aunt Louise died before she was thirty.
Because they are done away with,
they will never
cheer for any horse at any Kentucky Derby.
They will not root for the
come-from-behind underdog,
or praise the lone politician who
challenges the unchallengeable front runner.
Because they are done away with,
they will never
attempt to scribe a single word in any diary,
walk down the street to a newly
opened Starbucks,
or dance to music coming from
somebody's nearby radio.
Because they are done away with,
never will a single one of them

8^10 *(Eight to the Tenth Power)*

look at a photograph of anything,

mistakenly throw something new

onto a garbage truck,

or relocate from Osaka to Oklahoma City,

Paris to Perth, Savannah to Seattle.

Because they are done away with,

no member of this done-away-with group will

win the Nobel Prize for physics, literature, peace,

medicine or for any other Nobel category.

Nor will a single one of them be awarded the

Pulitzer for any well written newspaper story.

Because they are done away with,

there will be no Jim

knowing Keyshawn,

no Helen knowing Lucy, no Dixie knowing Lars,

no Dafinna knowing Karin,

no Lee knowing Stewart.

They will never have names, birth certificates,

drivers' licenses, or passports.

Because they are done away with,

never will any of them

think about the differences between Arab and Jew,
Korean and Japanese, Catholic and Buddhist,
Seven Day Adventist and Atheist, Saint and Sinner.

23

<u>Pause</u>

The Sage of Chugu-ji spoke with practiced crudeness
that betrayed wisdom, suffering, and sacrifice.
Always looking into Sorrow's eyes.
Always meditating upon the most pitiful,
the most disdainful; the most helpless:
those with no hope, little chance to survive.
Each day he knew more than he knew the day before.
And each nigh he slept on the mattress of his increased
knowledge.
He wanted most of all to find a way to end the useless
slaughtering
of the non-rebellious millions.
The millions who never lift a
finger, a voice, or utter
the slightest objection against their
killers.

8^10 *(Eight to the Tenth Power)*

Everyone, the world over,
but surely here in his homeland,
always shed tears at the mention of those
who did not survive the 1945 bombings of Hiroshima,
of Nagasaki.
The people always stop,
and peep into his small,
hardened-sand hut,
on the periphery of Chiyoda City,
asking him to offer a few words on peace,
forgiveness, beauty, kindness, truth.
Giving him a few yen just to say,
to promise, to make them believe
that there will never be another month like August 1945.
He is constantly perplexed, even as the Sage of Chugu-ji,
over how his countrymen can live so placidly
in these current times
when all around them, among them, with them,
are the cruel, the rich, the blind, the intelligent,
the callous, the benevolent, the vicious,
the peaceful, and the virtuous who consistently kill

that which they have not seen, heard, walked with;
and have not plotted or fought against.
Yes, he knew they must know that all around them there
are innocent deaths by the millions
who have died while not wronging a single human,
a single animal, or a single plant.
Have died while not voicing any words of hatred
towards individuals, institutions, or governments.
Still, these innocents, these fully without any sin,
are routinely slaughtered.
Yet, so many of his country's, young and old,
continue to ask about August 1945.
They want him, the Sage of Chugu-ji,
to offer words that will allay their anxieties
concerning future renderings of death,
while all around them and among them,
millions are being killed before they can ever
share one thought coming from the great
Siddhārtha Gautama: The Buddha.

24

On another continent, similar thoughts are being formed

8^10 *(Eight to the Tenth Power)*

about places with names that many still don't know
how to properly pronounce:
Treblinka, Majdanek, Sobibor, Auschwitz-Birkenau,
Belzec, Chelmno, Banjica, Flossenburg,
Gross-Rosen, Buchenwald,
Ravensbruck, Jasenovac, Sachsenhausen, Drancy, Dachau,
Bergen-Belsen.
These names:
That is why in the midst of cold nights,
on the island of Sylt,
between Deutschland and Denmark,
Herr Bauer
often looks across the forever chilled waters
of the North Sea,
where penetrating voices can be heard,
should one be quiet enough,
saying:
"Ich bin traurig und traurig. Traurig und traurig für die
ganze Deutschland
Bitte verzeihen Gott, uns all."
("I am sad and sorry. Sad and sorry

for all of Deutschland
Please, God, forgive us all.")
The ancient dead, who perished in the places
with "those names,"
Herr Bauer knows, are still
being mourned, cried over, grieved and deified.
But, the new dead?
Well?
The celebrated historians, with their history books;
and the pious sophists, with their
worshipping of bygone philosophers,
tell us only about the old ones.
The ones who perished at
Treblinka, Majdanek, Sobibor, Auschwitz-
Birkenau, Belzec, Chelmno, Banjica, Flossenburg, Gross-
Rosen, Buchenwald,
Ravensbruck, Jasenovac, Sachsenhausen, Drancy, Dachau,
Bergen-Belsen.
Whose offspring resides in places like
Jerusalem, Miami, Toronto, New York,
Haifa, Tel Aviv, Paris.

8^10 *(Eight to the Tenth Power)*

But it is the new dead,
the ones without any protective code or creed,
without any universal treaty,
without the International Red Cross,
without a commission sitting in the Hague,
without a Geneva Protocol.
These are the "New Ones" who are killed
without any peoples or countries
expressing sorrow, pity,
regret, shame, grief.
The "New Ones" are the ones ignored by
en vogue
humanitarians, who will hastily fly to
Port-au-Prince and Khartoum
to assist in the saving of poor dreams,
dreamt by
even poorer dreamers.
The executioners of the "New Ones" will never stand
before
Cour Internationale de Justice.
(The International Court of Justice)

CHESTER ALFONSO

The killers of the "New Ones" will not be pursued,
persecuted, and prosecuted
in places like Buenos Aires, Rio de Janeiro, and Detroit
for crimes committed against humanity.
Herr Bauer, though old,
remembers the massive killings:
Ending lives of those who had no machinery to fight back.
And, because of these memories, his daily prayer,
for more than 60-long-years,
has been in harmony with the probing
prayer he carries each night from
the voices of the North Sea:
"Ich bin traurig und traurig. Traurig und traurig für die
ganze Deutschland.
Bitte verzeihen Gott, uns all."
But, what prayer has Herr Bauer
and the voices of the North Sea
composed for the
"New Ones" that have been and are still being executed?
Executed,
not at Treblinka, Majdanek, Sobibor,

8^10 *(Eight to the Tenth Power)*

Auschwitz-Birkenau, Belzec
Chelmno, Banjica, Flossenburg, Gross-Rosen, Buchenwald
Ravensbruck, Jasenovac, Sachsenhausen, Drancy, Dachau,
Bergen-Belsen –
but in the state-of-art hospitals and homes of
Berlin, Frankfurt, Cologne, Munich,
Hamburg, Hanover, Dresden, Dusseldorf, Mainz,
and other places
steeped in modern architecture
and 21st century tolerance.
What prayer has Herr Bauer and the North Sea voices
composed for these innocents?

25

Pause

Someone brave enough has said:
"Not mine, you will not destroy mine.
Though I am too poor, undereducated,
and without good enough health
to properly care for
my new borne,
I will love this child with all the love any mother

can possibly love a child and I will protect this child
with every fiber of my own body.
I will give my all for this child,
even my own life.
Therefore, you will not destroy mine."
Someone strong enough has said:
"I will fight till the end of my days.
I will rush forward against your senseless
propaganda and promises.
I will not allow, ever, this life inside me to die
before he or she has a right to see a moon,
a sun, a hope;
to see and touch my face and be fed from my
breast. You may call me stupid,
a government dependent, a less-than-fortunate. The
big wheels and the little wheels and the rich folks
and the poor folks may ridicule me.
But, till my last breath is taken away,
I will, using all my power and strength,
give birth to my child.
And I will protect and care for this

8^10 *(Eight to the Tenth Power)*

child for as long as I shall live. So help me, God!"

26

How would you feel if you were told at conception
that you would never be able to
experience being noticed?
What about not having a chance to know
courage, perseverance,
or caring about losing or gaining weight?
And:
What about never having to worry or
rejoice about
getting a better grade, establishing a friendship,
getting a nice gift for a birthday present,
or the perfect marriage, the best holiday,
or the healthy life?
And:
How would you feel if you were told, at conception,
that you would be robbed of the chance to ever say,
"I love you?"
How would you feel if you were told, at conception,
that you would never see a star,

a grain of sand, falling snow flakes, or a smile?
How would you feel if you were told, at conception,
that you would never have to ponder
whether or not there is a God?

27

He knows the language.
He masters all the necessary
tools.
Words like: dilation and evacuation;
trimesters: first, second and third;
cervical dilation, laminaria, cervix,
forceps, and, uterine lining are as common
to him as the heat in his native Saudi Arabia.
Still, the words bother him. Always have.
After all, he is a deeply religious man.
It is this medical language that explains things like
how the suction catheter is inserted
to remove the baby's brain.
He understands words like:
prostaglandin and the
syringe with the spinal needle,

8^10 *(Eight to the Tenth Power)*

used to inject poison into the uterus;
thereby killing helpless life while it sleeps.
But, of all the medical and scientific understandings,
he best understands that he should always
obey the Noble Qur'an.
So, daily he prays that Allah will favorably
answer his prayers.
Still, how does he reconcile the Prophet's words with his
actions?
For, does not the Prophet say:
"And kill not your offspring for fear of poverty;
it is We Who provide for them and for you.
Surely, destroying them is a great sin."
If only the cost of studying medicine
at the University of Edinburgh
were not so great,
Najib Ahmed Shakir, thought,
then,
he would not have to perform these dreadful and
sinful acts.
Maybe, then, if the costs were less,

maybe he could find a
small but lavish apartment
in lovely Taormina, Sicily,
where he could rest on the white beaches
and swim in the clear
and warm waters of the Ionian Sea,
where he would continue his prayers to
Allah for forgiveness of his many sins.
The most egregious of these sins: the removal of
innocent life from grieving and desperate women.
He would always seek Allah's blessed rewards
and for his deliverance from hell and all evil.
Najib was troubled mostly by the women, the girls -
all Followers of the Prophet,
and always their complete silence
before he inserted the uterine curette
to scrape the uterus and remove the placenta,
making sure all life is scrubbed away,
terminated, eradicated.
Sometimes Najib killed the life by injecting the
syringe with the spinal needle.

8^10 *(Eight to the Tenth Power)*

So many of them:
Young girls, middle-aged women. All fearful.
All having been instructed by
Followers of the Prophet
not to say a single word concerning
who made them this way.
This always made it difficult for Najib.
He had studied at the University of Miami,
in Florida, the USA.
He was considered an outstanding physician:
specializing in the reproduction system of women.
Many years had passed since he had met his wife,
a Non-Believer,
who he had converted to Islam.
They had three children, all girls: ages 23, 24, and 26.
All studying to be doctors.
The costs were staggering,
even for a man like himself.
So, to make things easier,
he started, very slowly, at first,
for 5000 ر.س *(Saudi Riya),*

to end the pregnancies of a few,
wealthy and extremely discreet,
Saudi women.
Women with rich, powerful and prominent husbands
or well hidden, secret lovers.
Women, who had become pregnant,
they all claimed, by mistake.
Then, little by little, word about his illegal practice,
among the elite, spread.
Demands for his treatment multiplied ten-fold.
Fearing for his and his family's safety,
one day on a visit to London,
he, his wife and their three daughters decided to
never return to their home near the Red Sea.
So, it is here,
in the southern portion of this sin-filled city, London,
in Croydon,
that he performs this abhorrent medical procedure.
The same procedure those of lesser
faith and little remorse,
also perform.

8^10 *(Eight to the Tenth Power)*

And, because of this, he is able to provide
for his three daughters' education
at the ridiculously expensive
University of Edinburgh Medical School.
He was awaiting a new young woman,
very young he had been told.
Already this was the third operation of the day.
They came from all over,
these sweet, frightened,
Muslim girls and women.
Some were as young as fourteen;
one girl,
a mere child, was only eleven.
Those having enough courage to speak, claimed
their husbands or their benefactors had made
them this way by accident.
A few, showing even more courage, said they
had been raped or
had been bought and kept by wealthy men,
who perpetually used them
for the sexual acts the men's wives

or their special women would not perform.
Men who, to be certain, prayed daily to Allah.
Men who could recite the Qur'an verbatim
but who have no respect
for their veiled, subservient and obedient women.
The operating room was ready.
The instruments were in place; the table clean.
Najib removed his sandals,
fell to his knees, faced eastward, and prayed.

28

<u>Pause</u>

The old woman said:
"For as long as there's been human seed,
there have been those willing to remove and destroy that
seed: Life.
Always there are the willing killers, the salivating slayers,
the eager murderers, the avid extinguishers,
the ardent annihilators, the anxious erasers,
and the in-a-hurry abolishers of the seed: Life."
The smell of garlic kept escaping her mouth and
spicing each of her words:

8^10 *(Eight to the Tenth Power)*

"Without ever committing a sin,
the innocent seeds have been
canceled out, declared null and void,
dispensed with, obliterated, disposed of, terminated,
wiped away, outright killed, murdered.
Did that mad man of the East,
Genghis Khan,
massacre as many?
What about that power-hungry fool in Russia,
Stalin,
was he covered in as much innocent blood as this?
Or, that bastard, Hitler,
did his death chambers dispose of
as many innocent seeds as all of this?"
She paused for a short while and then she continued:
"There is never a memorial for these victims.
Never books written and fingers pointed at the
perpetrators,
at the executioners, the squelchers,
the undoers.
There are no movies with actors portraying these victims.

CHESTER ALFONSO

*No documentaries showing them being taken from a
small house on Amsterdam's Prinsengracht,
or from the ghetto streets of Prague, Heidelberg,
Budapest, or Sophia."*

Her words, mixed with her slobber, kept coming:

*"They have never had names, titles, bank accounts.
They've had no criminal records,
no high school transcripts, no addresses.
Their DNA has forever been abolished,
wiped away, liquidated.
Their fingerprints have been mangled
with their ground-up fingers, legs, and brains.
Their yells for assistance,
for someone,
for anyone to step forward, to offer a helping hand,
were too softly uttered to be heard."*

Bravely, still speaking softly, she continued:

*"None have had eye color, hair color, skin color.
They've not had shoe sizes, dress sizes, pant sizes,
any sizes.
They've had no favorite music, or book,*

8^10 *(Eight to the Tenth Power)*

or painting, or food, or hero.
They've never experienced a winter,
summer, spring, a fall,
a day or a night.
They've not had a desire to become greater
than they were or might be.
They've held no grudges, no dislikes,
no pride, no envy, no fears.
They've never imagined climbing Mount Everest,
or scuba diving off the coast of Guam.
Their lives were not complicated lives,
not hard lives, or good lives."

Then she stopped speaking.
Her face was frozen, it seemed, forever,
before she moved a single muscle.
The smell of the garlic had intensified.
She reached into her handbag,
resting on the small table next to her,
and withdrew a pencil and a piece of paper.
On the paper she wrote:

"8^10 = 1,073,741,824."

Then, she said:

"This is how many and the number keeps rising:

$8\wedge 10 = 1,073,741,824$

That is:

Eight to the tenth power.

This is:

One billion,

73 million,

741 thousand,

eight hundred and twenty-four."

The old lady passed the paper, with the numbers, to those concerned and patronizing enough to have remained, to have listened, and to have observed her silly ways.
The numbers were examined and then ridiculed, satirized, and finally, folded and placed in an envelope.
Copies of the note were soon forwarded to those who study these type things:

8^10 *(Eight to the Tenth Power)*

The renowned social scientists,

the Council of Churches,

the Organization of Islamic Cooperation,

the Holy See,

the United Nations' World Health Organization,

the U.S. Center for Disease Control,

and many more such

organizations.

After reviewing the old lady's claim,

They, as one, declared:

"This must be rejected.

How could there be such a large number?

Obviously, this foolish old lady is insane."

29

His had been a torturous journey:

Born to a Northern Ireland prostitute; abandoned by the

same prostitute.

Homeless at the age of six.

Institutionalized before turning ten.

Wandering between his fifteenth and twenty-first

birthdays

through most of North America
and then Europe.
Seldom, if ever, accompanied by anyone;
not even by other stragglers.
All the time believing misery, rejection,
loneliness, and dejection rested on his eyelids,
while torture and death, he always knew,
were only seconds away.
He had named himself after
the infamous poet, François Villon.
Telling those good-hearted enough and not afraid to ask,
that he was Frank Vill.
In a café in the German city of Mainz,
on the banks of the Rhine River,
Frank Vill,
one April morning, just before eleven a.m.,
held a conversation with a pale lady, of thirty-one.
A sad lady with a thin, sad face.
An even sadder smile
and much sadder eyes.
Her hands shook like those of a heroin addict in desperate

8^10 *(Eight to the Tenth Power)*

need of her next dose.
She appeared to be someone who continually carried
a suitcase
filled with pain, sorrow, misfortune, and destruction.
She spoke in a
dispirited, sorrowful, mournful, pleading manner
that Frank Vill recognized as the many voices he
had heard when, at the age of twelve,
he had witnessed young boys and girls
being sexual molested by older men so they,
the young boys and girls,
could scrape enough money to buy pieces of bread.
She told him, for years, she had been repeatedly abused -
over and over and over again -
by the man and woman she once worked for
as a cook, maid, and nanny.
The man and woman had kept her a prisoner in their
lavish mansion in the Blankenese Süllberg Hill
sector of Hamburg,
overlooking the Elbe.
This man,

with his wife in attendance, and happily participating,

had engaged her sexually whenever they so desired;

starting back when she was fifteen.

They had even posted security guards

and installed anti-escape security devices

to ensure she remained their prisoner and sex toy.

Then, she said, she was beautiful, intelligent and Christian.

Now, she is physically, mentally, and emotionally ruined.

She told Frank Vill that she no longer believes

in the Pope, Luther, the Saints,

or any force claiming to offer relief for those in misery;

for those possessing

the scars of unimaginable degradation and pain.

Casually, she touched and continually

caressed Frank Vill's

hands, then she would squeeze them, gently.

Looking deeply into his eyes,

she told him she believed he could make

all the bad things in her mind disappear;

and, so doing, all the horrible events,

whatever they might be,

8^10 *(Eight to the Tenth Power)*

in his life, would also be made to disappear.
Still looking deeply into his eyes,
she told him she would
demonstrate all the things she had learned
as the rich couple's cook,
maid, nanny, prisoner and whore.
She would do things to him and for him,
pleasurable things, so pleasing,
that they, the things she would do,
would make him weep with happiness.
Would make him feel as if all the joys of the world
were flowing through his veins.
After days of caressing her pale skin,
nourishing her with calming words,
after lengthy walks
through Wiesbaden's Kurpark,
after hearing her sighs as she pressed against him,
breathed onto him,
he decided that he had to act.
Had to avenge what had
happened to them both,

albeit,

in different places and by different people.

So, he read book after book;

watched rented movies,

practiced relentlessly.

After several months of dedicated

and devoted mental and physical preparation,

Frank Vill knew he was ready for their mission.

The rich doctor's maid, cook, nanny, prisoner,

and forced to be whore, had convinced him

that they must violate God's Sixth Commandment:

The one having to do with killing.

30

When they are removed

they will not breath, see, smell, feel;

they will not know about taste,

nor will they ever know what it is like not to know.

And,

when they are demolished

they will be gone forever from Earth;

never to be moved by a violin's sound,

8^10 *(Eight to the Tenth Power)*

or ask why there are traffic jams in Reykjavik.

And,

because they are wiped away, there will be

fewer mouths to feed,

clothes to buy,

and fewer visits to pediatricians.

31

The sign read:

"Liquidation sale.

Getting rid of everything in stock.

No questions asked.

No refunds.

No regrets.

Closing for good.

Once all stock is gone, we're gone."

Someone said,

" Ok, let's neutralize this situation.

Get it over with.

No use keeping what we don't need, don't want.

Let's cut-bait and haul-ass outta here.

We've always been sour on the damn thing.

Get rid of the whole shebang.
There are already too many of these things anyway.
Everywhere you look you see one.
What were we thinking?
Who in the hell thought of this in the first place?
Hope everybody is happy with the decision to
liquidate. If you are not, too bad,
'cause that's what we are about to do."

32

They,
all of them,
have been prevented,
forever, from
walking down Shanghai's Nanjing Lu,
having lunch at Four Seasons des Bergues Geneva,
or drinking tea
at Cafe Le Hobbit, Quebec City.
These are the ones whose feet will never
touch any soil or get frost bite in any winter.
They will never catch a glimpse of a Lunar Eclipse.
Nor will they taste a strawberry or chocolate milkshake.

8^10 *(Eight to the Tenth Power)*

There will not be, for them,

smiles at anyone's wedding or tears at any sad movie.

They will not ask anyone for street directions.

Nor will any of them worry about a son

or daughter not returning safely from any war.

33

Fifty/ maybe 100/ 200/ maybe, even a billion.

Is there anybody counting?

Who cares? Who gives a damn?

34

Who are these

life-enders?

Who are these erasers of potential greatness?

They are,

to be sure,

from every country, maybe, even, the Vatican.

They speak every language,

verbally or in sign.

They're educated, ignorant, illiterate, well read.

Some are humble. Others are arrogant.

They are the loud, profane and the boastful,

as well as the quite, profound and the shy.
These are city people, small town people,
farm people, village people.
They are the people who travel the world, and
the people who have never left their hometowns.
Some work with their hands,
some with their feet, some with their minds.
Some analyze, others manipulate.
Some see the big picture, others have never seen a picture.
Some borrow and never pay back.
Some drive trains, pluck corn,
sew shirts, slice tomatoes, build cars, repair worn shoes.
They come from every part of life:
doctors, tennis players, teachers, ballerinas, social workers,
students, the unemployed, street people, movie stars,
scientists, welfare recipients, wealthy philanthropists,
morticians, waitress, police, race car drivers,
black jack dealers, trash collectors,
nurses, landscapers, secretaries, prostitutes, soldiers,
sailors, Marines, airmen,
writers, tap-dancers, chefs, meteorologists, care

8^10 *(Eight to the Tenth Power)*

givers, boat operators, strollers along Mexico City avenues.
And the list continues:
They are maids, gardeners, ministers, singers, politicians,
stealers of union dues,
coal miners, auto salespeople, hair cutters, hair stylists,
the homeless, Fifth Avenue residents,
television personalities,
grocery store clerks, fashion models,
fashion designers, fashion promoters, shoe shiners,
airplane pilots, psychologists, picture framers,
and picture takers;
church folks and folks
who've never seen the inside of a church;
revolutionaries, subway harmonica players,
bed-pan-emptying LPNs,
Olympic winners, Olympic losers, mothers, daughters,
grandmothers, single mothers, married mothers,
aunts, nieces, cousins, grown-before-their-time little girls,
granddaughters, wives, next door neighbors,
pole-dancers, girlfriends,
members of the Daughters of the American Revolution;

CHESTER ALFONSO

Eastern Star women,
cocktail waitresses; professors of history, literature,
physics, whatever.
They hail from Peru, France, Tonga, Panama, China,
Cook Island, Samoa, Svalbard, Bulgaria, Serbia,
Cyprus, Argentina, Chad, San Marino, Slovakia,
Ukraine, Vanuatu, Fiji, Brunei,
Burkina Faso, Canada, Portugal, Brazil, South Africa,
Mexico, Macao, Georgia, Ethiopia, Bangladesh,
Australia, Liechtenstein, the Philippines, Taiwan,
Saint Lucia, Paraguay, Andorra, Jordan, Botswana,
Maldives, Lebanon, Togo, Zambia, Bolivia, Iraq,
Mongolia, Ukraine, Yemen, Palau, Tajikistan,
Turkmenistan, Singapore, Pakistan, Switzerland,
Victoria, Canada; Oporto, Portugal; Madagascar,
Victoria, Seychelles; Phnom Penh, Cambodia,
Bamako, Mali, Kyrgyzstan, Suriname,
and from towns, cities, and postal codes
throughout the United States of America,
and every other place where human conception occurs.
From all the nations they have come

8^10 *(Eight to the Tenth Power)*

and will continue coming.
Some crying and begging for forgiveness,
others asking for nothing.
Many are braggart and defiant,
others are meek and compliant.
There are the ones who are protected by the law
and the ones who will never be protected by any law.
Who are these folk?
Well, these folks profess belief in
Hinduism, Islam, Taoism, Judaism, Sikhism,
Buddhism, Baha'i', Christianity, Confucianism,
Rastafarianism, Shintoism, Babism; some are agnostic,
some atheist, some are downright lowlife.
They belong to sororities like:
Zeta Phi Omega, Alpha Sigma Tau,
Alpha Delta Pi, Chi Omega,
Delta Gamma, Alpha Kappa Alpha,
Alpha Xi Delta, Phi Omega Sigma,
Omega Phi Delta, Omega Phi Alpha, Epsilon Sigma Alpha,
Alpha Phi Omega.
Their parents gave them names

to match the beauty of their birth:
Gloria, Jasmine, Dorothy, Helen,
MaryAnn, Judith, Maria, Tiffany,
Yvonne, Juanita, Betty, Evelyn, Kimberly,
Lacey, Lauren, Olivia,
Abigail, Madalynn, Camino, Gezana,
Julita, Mahogony, Caria,
Bianca, Allison, Rachael, Ursala, Henriqua, Adie,
Wilhelmina, Suki,
Edina, Mariko, Redhiya, Fang,
Chizuko, Tamako, Bertina, Freda
Edeline, Liese, Zhuo, Niu, Dao-Ming,
Lei, Pippin, Herta, Brynna,
Chiyoko, Bahati, Hua, Mei-Xing,
Selda, Elfrida, Gertrude, Alvar,
Seiko, Chika, Kamie, Halle, Winola,
Akako, Lian, Fugo, Sanura,
And, the millions of other names
matching the wonderment of their first sighs.
All languages are represented by this group:
Lithuanian, Oromo, Turkish, French,

8^10 *(Eight to the Tenth Power)*

Hindi, Polish, Hausa,
Xhosa, Greek, Bengali, Wu, Tagalog,
Russian, Gan, Dutch,
Telugu, Armenian, Tibetan,
Arabic, Romanian, Korean,
Oriya, Fula, English, Cantonese,
Persian, Kongo, Thai,
Mandarin, German, Hungarian,
Malay, Italian, Somali, Hebrew,
Kurdish, Indonesian, Spanish,
Japanese, Vietnamese, Punjabi,
and the thousands of other tongues
that will prevent emerging life
from ever singing, hearing, or patting feet to a single song.
Who are these folks?
Well,
these folks have two things in common:
They are all female, and
they have the audacity and power to allow
the termination, rejection, disposition,
wasting, and mutilation

of a life,

for reasons, they say,

are too varied, too complicated, too private

and too emotional

to be explained, or to be understood.

Alas,

many of these audacious females,

but not their supporters,

just might recall the day their legs were splayed apart,

and

some unique creation;

a portion of their flesh, blood and breath -

even though it had lived for a short time -

was removed forever

from them.

It will not matter how many more

times a similar creation occurs,

these audacious females will always remember

the creation they refused to see, to hold,

to play with, to nurse, to teach,

to love, to nurture, to say: "This is my child."

8^10 *(Eight to the Tenth Power)*

And, in their remembrance, they probably will not smile.

35

Somehow,

on some day,

someone will discover the meaning

of Birth, of Death,

of Alive, of Dead,

of Here, of Gone;

of Past Tense, Present Tense, Future Tense.

And, they will attempt applying significance to

What Could Have Been,

and

What Might Have Been

before someone, having a *"Choice,"*

decided to toss

Something Real, Something Bearing Life

into a toilet stool or a drainage ditch.

Decided to forego patience.

Patience:

that commodity most

animals of the wild possess.

But the "Life-Enders" believe,
there are better things to do than to
wait a little while longer.
What joy, they surmise, is there
in waiting on the things that some say are important
but others know to be debilitating?
Why be patient, they surmise, when there is no
chance the outcome will cause anything
but trauma and pain?
Who has the calculator, the machine that
adds, multiplies, subtracts, divides –
that does the math and
tell us how many slaughtered fetus
is worth a mother's happiness?
Why be patient when the only thing to be patient for
is the essence of an
unimaginable and beautiful happening:
Bringing forth a new life?
Patience:
That strength God so diligently demonstrated by
making all else before creating Man.

8^10 *(Eight to the Tenth Power)*

36

The young, well, relatively young, doctor

at the Capital Reproduction Center,

long ago had philosophically and spiritually

declared allegiance with the

poor, the exploited, the confused.

Allegiance with those who have few alternatives,

and little or no way of coping with life's

most beautiful,

but sometimes, terrifying, dilemma.

Those, who, because of some mistake –

they often claim –

find

themselves in "this way:"

They:

These very poor, these too ignorant,

these too young, these too old and too confused.

They:

The ones not financially,

mentally, or emotionally prepared.

Already, far too many of them

suffering with debilitating physical and mental illnesses;

an abusive husband, boyfriend;

a closed-minded mother, father.

Their options:

Life, death, ostracism, acceptance,

change of lifestyle,

or

do what has been done by others in similar circumstances:

Never miss a beat. Get rid of the damn thing.

To hell with it.

Rationalizing:

This is only one out of a million, out of a hundred million.

Rationalizing:

This is my first time. This is my last time.

Rationalizing:

With seven billion folks already on the planet,

who needs another mouth to feed?

Who needs another polluter?

Rationalizing:

The world does not need another potential criminal.

Rationalizing:

8^10 *(Eight to the Tenth Power)*

Anyway, nobody will miss this one.

Rationalizing:

Look, it really doesn't matter, does it?

Rationalizing:

Everyone else is doing it.

Rationalizing:

I was just notified by my agent
that I have this audition for this fantastic part in a movie.
I can't possibly pass on this opportunity.

Rationalizing:

Like, who is going to know?

Rationalizing:

We can't afford another one.

Rationalizing:

It's Sam's fault. Told'em I wasn't on the pill.
Told'em him to withdraw before he climaxed.

Rationalizing:

You helped Sarah get rid of the one she was carrying.

Rationalizing:

Even the White House supports a woman's right to choose.

I'm just choosing. Nothing more. Nothing less.

CHESTER ALFONSO

This is my choice. My body.
And, the young doctor philosophizing:
The ones gotten rid of, the ones I abort,
are the ones
who will never be in any terrible, ugly,
and violent relationship for any reason.
Philosophizing
They will never be an additional burden on society.
Philosophizing:
They will never wish they were never born
while someone abuses them.
Philosophizing:
They will never join a street gang, sell dope,
be on welfare, join the military,
go to prison, or become serial killers.
Philosophizing:
They will never have too many messed-up kids that must
be taken care of by someone else.
So, the young, well, relatively young, doctor,
at the Capital Reproduction Center,
who long ago having philosophically and spiritually

8^10 *(Eight to the Tenth Power)*

declared allegiance with the
very poor, the confused ...
continued to remove fetus, after fetus, after fetus.
He no longer subscribes to that part of the
Hippocratic Oath that says:
"I will give no deadly medicine to any one if asked, nor suggest any such counsel; and similarly I will not give a woman a pessary to cause an abortion."
His new mantra: "Never miss a beat.
Get rid of as many of the damn things as possible."

37

The aborted ones
will never go online searching for a list of restaurants,
or have to wash clothes at a neighborhood laundry mat
while wondering if they have enough dimes, quarters
to deposit in the washer, in the dryer.
The aborted ones
will never have to endure anyone's stare
or tell a patient they have an incurable disease.
They will never have high blood pressure from thinking
about how they will make their

monthly mortgage payments.

These are the ones

who will never see, hear, or speak to a brother,

a sister, a cousin,

a mother, a father, a grandparent, a neighbor,

a police officer, a minister, a hair stylists, a rock star.

These are the ones

who will not be given a free ticket, promoted ahead of,

honored with a Purple Heart, a Badge of Courage,

or chosen homecoming queen; captain of any team.

These are the ones

nobody will ever mourn, celebrate, employ, castigate,

imprison, put in an embarrassing situation, bribe,

call a liar, an ignoramus,

or a good-for-nothing underachiever.

These are the ones who will never

be any of the things worth being.

They will forever be without all of this and any of that;

without few or many;

without rising or falling.

The aborted ones will be

8^10 *(Eight to the Tenth Power)*

without dreams of pleasure, pain, future,

past, success, failure –

without dreaming any dream.

38

There were two things Father John Anthony Macroy knew

were unshakable:

His love of God and his love of sex with women.

He was fifty-seven years old, with a head covered with

dark-brown hair

and filled with too much knowledge.

When he was twenty-nine he had been ordained, by the

Catholic Church, as a priest.

John Anthony Macroy's rise to parish priest,

of this quaint and beautiful city,

had somehow increased his love of God

as well as his desire for sex

with many of the town's devoutly Catholic women.

Indeed, his desire for sex multiplied

with his age and power.

Many of the middle-aged women,

along with some young, well scrubbed, catholic girls,

called him, in private, "Father Macjoy."
Even the nuns who assisted him were not off limits.
He would, for hours, pray with them:
Passionately immersed in reverent supplication
to the Holy Savior.
He would remind them how the Holy Savior
had given His only Son for
mankind's sins.
Then, as if hypnotized,
these women would succumb to his roving hands.
Later, confused and filled with shame,
they, these women,
would gather their clothing, hurry from his room,
reciting prayer after prayer as they sped
down the church's aisles,
their vulva on fire and throbbing
from the humongous thing hanging
between Father Macroy's legs.
None believed they could ever be forgiven
for what they had allowed to take place.
Still, many would return time and time again,

8^10 *(Eight to the Tenth Power)*

as if addicted to the good priest's love-making.
Father Macroy had never understood
the chasm between his
compulsive need for sex and his devotion to God.
A chasm most priests obeyed and never attempted to
hurdle.
No, he always felt the urge
to keep trying to satisfy his insatiable
and immense sexual appetite
with any woman and every woman he could.
He truly believed God had given him an over-sized sex
organ and inhuman sexual stamina
for the sole purpose of satisfying women
in desperate need of carnal satisfaction.
And, over the years,
not one of the women had officially complained.
Indeed, many had begged him to continue
his penetration and stretching of the
pleading slit resting between their thighs.
So, in his late forties,
more sagacious, more loving, more compassionate,

more spiritual than ever;
loved by so many,
he enticed the highly obedient Sister Elizabeth into his
chambers and onto his small bed.
Though, in all her years, she had twice masturbated,
she had never been sexually entwined
with another human being.
However, over the next several years,
Sister Elizabeth was had with abandonment.
Whatever his imagination, she acquiesced.
Each of her orifices were his to use as he saw fit.
And, the Good Sister, a willing subject,
had even acquired the language of
wanton passion and the mannerisms
of one possessing delirious sexual cravings.
Soon she worship Father Macroy as much as she
worshipped the Holy Savior.
And, so doing, she designed lascivious sexual activities
and experiments that led to even more desire for deeper
and broader satisfaction of the flesh.
The both of them:

8^10 *(Eight to the Tenth Power)*

Father Macroy and Sister Elizabeth,

when engaged in their torrid and salacious actions,

lost all reference to the Church, to the Holy Savior.

One year stretched into four and four into seven.

Seemingly overnight the once pure Sister Elizabeth

reached the age of thirty-six.

She, started to appreciate too much food.

After so many years, on the same bed,

in the same room, with the same man,

her sexual variety and creativity

became redundant, predictable, boring.

She simply could not think of any new positions

or types of performance

that still brought Father Macroy

the satisfaction she knew he so much deserved.

Too soon for Sister Elizabeth,

the good Father,

began to find her no longer attractive, desirable.

The humungous device,

hanging nearly to his knees,

was no longer stirred by any of their inventions.

CHESTER ALFONSO

Lord, knows, she did all she could to arouse him.
But, lo and behold, none of her efforts caused the slightest
increase in his desire for her buttocks,
her mouth, hands, or cunt.
Because of this, he persuaded her to find a replacement.
Bring him someone new, young, and fresh;
someone who had never
imagined being penetrated.
And, she did:
Within weeks her spot on Father Macroy's small bed
was supplanted by a shy,
much younger, Sister Denise.
And, like Sister Elizabeth,
Sister Denise spent many exhilarating hours upon that bed.
The one pushed against the wall
in Father Macroy's small room,
where he used and misused her timid body
with the same diligence he had
used and misused Sister Elizabeth's.
He continued to say the prayers.
And, he always studied and examined

8^10 *(Eight to the Tenth Power)*

the Books of the New Testament.
And, because he so well understood Latin,
he was always puzzled when Sister Denise,
in the throes of an intense orgasm,
would always scream, in Latin:
'Paenitentiam agite adpropinquavit
enim regnum caelorum."
(Repent: for the kingdom of heaven is at hand.)
Then, one day – it was a Thursday –
many flashing lights
were seen in front of and
on the side streets surrounding
the Catholic church housing the small bed in
Father Macroy's clean room.
A room filled, on this Thursday morning,
with the blood of three God-loving people.
The authorities
found papers, notes, diaries,
manuscripts, and other documents.
Father Macroy and Sister Elizabeth,
in their own handwritten words ,

had left behind a large three-ring binder
outlining how hundreds of women,
several nuns included,
had succumbed to the Father's great mind,
sincere smile, roving hands and huge cock.
Women who had relinquished their bodies,
souls, emotions, and respectabilities.
There was the diary entitled:
"Mortuus Fruges Voluptas,"
explaining how he, Father Macroy,
and later, Sister Elizabeth, had personally,
gone into women's uteruses -
with medical know-how,
and skillfully removed fetuses.
The diary told how they had expertly
used the spinal needle,
the vacuum aspiration, and the crochet.
Lying on the floor, in their blood,
were Sister Elizabeth, Sister Denise, and Father Macroy.
On the bed were embryotomy scissors,
forceps, uterine curettes,

8^10 *(Eight to the Tenth Power)*

plastic sheets, several bed pans, bottles of salves,
and bags filled with pain pills.
In a corner chair, in a small tub, were two dead fetuses.
Each with a note attached:
The note on one fetus read: "Puer Number Viginti"
The note on the other read: "Puer Number Viginti-unus"
There were many hours of investigating,
looking, probing,
and uneasy discussions with the cardinal bishop, the
janitor and others.
Then, a young detective, by the name of Henri Davidson,
noticed a slither of light coming through a crack,
that had been covered by a small, inexpensive rug,
under Father Macroy's small bed;
the one that still had the scent
and ugliness of tainted human blood and death.
A trap door.
That is what young Detective Davidson found.
Lifting the door and crawling into the small space,
the slim detective, holding a flashlight,
knew he had entered hell when he saw the stacks of flesh.

The piles looking like old,

moistureless, chopped liver.

There were cakes of dried blood everywhere.

The once secret dungeon was black

from the morbid, despicable remains of wasted life.

Tiny pieces of flesh were plastered on four walls.

All the skinny detective could say was: "Sweet, Jesus!"

39

They will never debate the pros and cons

of living near an ocean, close to an inactive volcano,

or being a vegetarian.

They will not debate the pluses or minuses of being

a member of Spain's Basque Separatist Group,

or of getting married before the age of eighteen.

They will never spend a Sunday morning

getting ready for church and thinking about having

a casual brunch afterwards.

They will never try explaining

the sudden death of a pet fish.

They will never wonder what lie

to tell a policeman who stops

8^10 *(Eight to the Tenth Power)*

them because they were driving too fast.
They will never sit in a library, in Manila,
trying to impress anyone by reading
"War and Peace," in Russian.
They will never try on a dress at a high-class,
way-too-expensive boutique,
or sing off-key while taking a shower.
They will never play with other children,
eat a meal at any café,
speak to any person living next door,
make a sand castle while relaxing on Zuma Beach,
or kiss anyone under a mistletoe on Christmas morning.
They will never have a first, middle or last name,
go to a dentist to have a tooth worked on,
have a picture taken for the high school's yearbook,
or be told they are too late to board a departing cruise ship.
They will never attend any grand opening.
Will never cheer for Manchester United, the Miami Heat,
the Bayi Rockets,
or the Arabian American Little League Baseball Team.
They will not be moved by the lyrics

of *Suicidios de Famosos*,
or read anything written by
Garcia Marquez.
They will never,
in cold months, apply Vicks Vapor Rub to
their chests,
pay a fine for being illegally parked,
spill paint on a new carpet,
fall in love with and get married to the wrong person,
or do whatever they fancy, with whomever they fancy,
anyway they fancy.
The ones who fail to survive
will never shovel snow
in Pueblo, Colorado or in Nagano, Japan.
They will not take the 10-hour train ride
From Melbourne's Spencer Station to
Sydney's Central Station.
They will not drink glasses of warm beer
in the University Of Wisconsin's Rathskeller
and then stagger down State Street
holding hands with a new, one-night-stand lover.

8^10 *(Eight to the Tenth Power)*

40

Elijah Sperm and millions of his siblings,
all so tiny,
were lost in a place they had never imagined;
fighting during their journey,
wading through troubled mush.
So many of them. Most, nearly all,
not surviving, falling by the wayside.
But, there was Elijah Sperm, gaining strength
from the cries of his dying brothers and sisters.
Pushing forward.
Leaving *Vagina*.
Heading to a place called: *Uterus*.
His arms, legs, lungs aching.
His mind clouded and confused.
Still, he was determined.
He had to continue.
He had to survive and make it to *Uterus*.
Ralph Sperm, the one with a sense of humor,
who made others laugh,
had fallen behind;

his jokes could no longer be heard.

Had he perished?

Had the journey been too strenuous for Ralph?

Maybe he'd spent too much time being a prankster

and not carefully watching his route.

Finally, too tired to breathe and completely exhausted,

almost falling by the wayside,

Elijah Sperm arrived at his destination: *Uterus*.

He was elated. Tired but happy.

Yet, he was sad.

None of his friends, who started down the path,

were with him.

He was alone, extremely fatigued, but so very blessed.

He tried to sleep

but was awakened by a resounding voice,

saying:

"Wake up, Elijah Sperm,

you may be tired but your voyage has not yet ended.

You have been blessed to make it this far without damage.

Now,

you must use all your strength and go to a new place.

8^10 *(Eight to the Tenth Power)*

This new place goes by the name, *Fallopian Tube*.
Once you arrive at *Fallopian Tube*,
you will have a pre-arranged holiday:
a period for reflection, rest, and recovery.
At *Fallopian Tube*, you will await a special friend.
This special friend is called *Ovulation*.
Once *Ovulation* arrives, it will join you.
At this point the journey is nearly over.
While you and *Ovulation* become acquainted,
the two of you will soon be joined by a *Mister Egg*.
Upon meeting *Mister Egg*,
you will come together as one.
And, from that coming together a thing many know as
Blastocyst, will form.
Blastocyst, which you will now
be part of, will soon create what some refer to as *Fetus*
others call it *Life*.
This *Fetus*; this *Life*,
will be followed by joy, happiness.
And you, Elijah Sperm,
having so valiantly survived, will be forever a hero."

41

There were numerous events scheduled.
Her calendar included attending concerts
and an upcoming wedding.
She was also excited about a possible career move,
maybe a big promotion.
The stars were aligned properly.
She was a kind, loving, smart, and beautiful young lady.
Weeks later, as promised,
the career move and the accompanying,
big promotion took place. She was thrilled.
She recalled how it started:
One Sunday, in June, with a co-worker,
she had gone to a *Three Tenors* Concert:
the best concert, the critics said,
ever to be held in Cleveland.
She met a new guy: One with money, power,
looks, a superb education.
No up-and-coming young lady
could have hoped for anything more.
And, then, she felt something was not right.

8^10 *(Eight to the Tenth Power)*

Her body was talking to her.//
Sending alert warnings.//
And, lo and behold, she missed another period.//
She purchased the pregnancy kit at a pharmacy –//
far from her own neighborhood.//
She set nervously on her bathroom's toilet stool,//
let some of her pee flow into the drinking glass,//
placed the strip into the glass,//
and watched as the two bands started to show.//
Walking down Euclid Avenue,//
not far from the Ernst and Young Building,//
she was nearly frozen.//
She was always smiling. Always happy. Never afraid.//
Always believing in this thing called "Karma."//
Always knowing people would reap what they had sowed.//
The thirty-three year-old state representative, Leven,//
the man she had met at the *Three Tenors* Concert, that//
Sunday, back in June,//
had made her feel like a new woman.//
She was certain he had//
intervened to get her the Ernst and Young job

and the promotion.

Each time he drove up from Columbus,

they had spent precious hours

holding and loving each other.

She had known before they ever made love – months ago,

that he was supposedly happy in marriage.

That he had two young children: a boy and a girl.

His wife had graduated from

a very prestigious university in Michigan.

Further down Euclid,

at a chic coffee shop,

she extracted the cell phone from her purse

and telephoned

the Planned Parenthood's Shaker Heights office.

She made an appointment for November 25,

the day before Thanksgiving.

42

Now, Frank Vill

stood across the road from the

Christianeum Hamburg Gymnasium.

The rich man's maid, cook, nanny, prisoner,

8^10 *(Eight to the Tenth Power)*

and forced-to-be whore,
was behind the wheel of the stolen Opel Corsa,
bearing Munich license plates.
She was ready and
anxious to purge herself of the possessive hatred and
evil memories that always accompanied her.
The tall boy was handsome and athletic.
She had raised, nurtured and played with him.
He was slightly slouched in his stance.
His long blond hair - covering his eyes and ears –
was blowing.
He saw the family driver approaching
and removed his backpack.
Then, suddenly his future ended.
His iPod fell to the ground.
Blood quickly covered both the backpack and the iPod.
Doctor Helmut Schmitz
was in the process of performing yet another abortion.
His eyes, his hands, his mind, his reasoning,
as usual, were steady and focused.
Then, Nurse Gilda

ran into the room.
She was crying, shaking, almost unable to speak:
"Herr Doctor Schmitz, Rikard,
your son, they say he has been shot."
Nowadays, the wealthy Herr Doctor Schmitz,
an outstanding member of Hamburg's elite,
rarely leaves his study,
not even to eat his meals.
Not even to perform special
operations on women who are consumed with getting
rid of their future children.
No longer does he hold conversations,
watch television, listen to music.
However, he is ashamed to admit, his loins still ache
when he thinks of the former cook, maid,
and nanny;
the whore, who was their prisoner.
The girl who came to him as a mere child; fifteen, she was.
Her stomach already beginning
to show the signs of the pregnancy.
Some Turkish hoodlum, in St. Pauli,

8^10 *(Eight to the Tenth Power)*

she claimed, had raped and abused her.
She was repulsed by the though of having a Turk's child.
So, Herr Doctor Schmitz,
the proud father of a newborn son,
worked his magic:
Erasing all signs of any pregnancy.
Then, weeks later, he saw her,
as he and his wife were leaving the Tsao Yang Restaurant,
in the Kempinski Hotel Atlantic.
She smiled and then spoke with him and his wife,
telling them she was without money
and no place to stay.
They offered her a job and a room.
She would be their housekeeper and nanny.
And, soon, a few months later,
Fraulein Deltra became "Deltra-the-in-house-whore;"
and their prisoner.
Frau Schmitz, to be sure,
enjoyed Deltra much more than the pompous Doctor.
But, it was Herr Doctor who made her pregnant four times.
And, four times Herr Doctor

removed from her the bits and pieces of a child.
Each time a smiling Frau Schmitz
held Deltra's shaking hands,
wiped away Deltra's tears, while passionately
French kissing Deltra's mouth and squeezing her breast.
Fraulein Deltra, since her ingenious escape,
has never left Herr Doctor Schmitz's mind.
Not even after this terrible tragedy;
this uncivilized and barbaric act
against his son and the entire - most honored –
Schmitz's family.
The Schmitzs:
one of Hamburg's finest families;
owners of high-end real estate throughout
the Hamburg region.
Despite the two million euro reward
and the assistance of Europe's finest
law enforcement agencies,
the shooter had never been identified;
not a single hint or lead.
Rumors were rampant about a Turkish gangster and

8^10 *(Eight to the Tenth Power)*

a Roma, maybe, even, some stupid German.
Two years nothing but grief,
pain, loneliness, remorsefulness.
The questions the Schmidtzs ask,
each moment, of each waken hour, of each day:
"Why would anyone destroy
a life before it has a chance to enjoy its future?
Why take the life of such an innocent
and beautiful boy with so much to give?
What have we done to deserve this?
Why has God been so cruel, so unkind?
Why has God destroyed our lives?"

43

In her new *"Always Hot Like Hell's Suppose to Be"* home,
Margaret is forever smiling, peacocking,
and filled with bliss.
She is one of Lucifer's favorites. One of his brightest.
Even the other repugnant, abhorrent dwellers
have finally recognized and applauded her life's work.
Her diligent devotion and dedication
to the elimination of those unworthy and

unfit for the place where they, these abhorrent dwellers,
once patrolled: Earth.
It does not matter that, in her previous world's life,
she, like many of the other occupants of the specially
designed *"Elite Dormitory,"*
had been ridiculed, criticized, imprisoned,
labeled racist, sinner, despot,
Nazi, anti-religionist, murderer, and hater of the poor.
Now, all those around her,
sitting on their always burning-charcoaled benches,
in this world of the despicable and forever damned,
appreciate and rejoice at their
association with Saint Sanger.
Her work has won her a place in the highest,
most elite realm of this most repugnant, evil,
fire-filled cavern,
where she oftentimes rub elbows with the Ruler,
Lucifer, himself.
On occasion Lucifer,
the demon and ruler of The Fallen, bring forth
all the inhabitants of the Elite Dormitory,

8^10 *(Eight to the Tenth Power)*

and, before them all,
he gives praise to the wonderful Saint Margaret Sanger.
In her spare moments she
exchange views, have discussions with some of the worst
characters to have ever walked upon the planet Earth.
This is when they debate the many methods
of genocide, murder, eugenics,
ethnic cleansing, and population control.
And, always, the eradication of the
weak so the strong can better survive.
The participants, auguring the finer points,
most often include:
Misters Hitler, Lenin, and Stalin;
Misters Genghis Khan, Mao Zedong, and Pol Pot;
Misters Idi Amin, Saddam Hussein, and Hideki Tojo;
and, Misters Augusto Pinochet,
Francois "Papa Doc" Duvalier, Jonas Savimbi.
Also,
Misters Leopold II, Benito Mussolini, Slobodan Milosevic;
as well as,
Misters Omar al-Bashir, Ivan the Terrible,

Jean Kambanda and Kim II Sung.

Sometimes,

another woman, Pauline Nyiramasuhuko,

will join in the debates.

Saint Sanger frequently recites her two favorite stories:

How Hillary's words

once moved her to tears.

And, how Martin's words shook her

like she had never before been shaken.

How Hillary had, so eloquently, said:

"The 20th century reproductive rights movement, really

embodied in the life and leadership of Margaret Sanger,

was one of the most transformational in the entire history

of the human race. It has changed the lives of tens of

millions of women. It has changed attitudes and

perceptions about

women and our roles in society. It ushered in demographic

and social changes that have brought us closer to gender

equality than at any time.

8^10 *(Eight to the Tenth Power)*

"Yet we know that Margaret Sanger's work here in the United States and certainly across our globe is not done. Here at home, there are still too many women who are denied their rights because of income, because of opposition, because of attitudes that they harbor. But around the world, too many women are denied even the opportunity to know about how to plan and space their families. They're denied the power to do anything about the most intimate of decisions.

"And the derivative inequities that result from all of that are evident in the fact that women and girls are still the majority of the world's poor, unschooled, unhealthy, and underfed. This is and has been for many years a matter of personal and professional importance to me, and I want to assure you that reproductive rights and the umbrella issue of women's rights and empowerment will be a key to the foreign policy of this Administration."

And, Saint Sanger always bore them with her constant and verbatim recitation of words written by the great Martin, which were delivered, at the award ceremony, by his wife, Coretta:

"There is a striking kinship between our movement and Margaret Sanger's early efforts. She, like we, saw the horrifying conditions of ghetto life. Like we, she knew that all of society is poisoned by cancerous slums. Like we, she was a direct actionist — a nonviolent resister. She was willing to accept scorn and abuse until the truth she saw was revealed to the millions. At the turn of the century she went into the slums and set up a birth control clinic, and for this deed she went to jail because she was violating an unjust law. Yet the years have justified her actions. She launched a movement which is obeying a higher law to preserve human life under humane conditions. Margaret Sanger had to commit what was then called a crime in order to enrich humanity, and today we honor her courage and vision; for without them there would have been no beginning."

8^10 *(Eight to the Tenth Power)*

They, especially Misters Hitler and Pol Pot,
always applaud her tenacity, courage, and passion
to eliminate those who could and would pollute the
"Better Society."
They always shower her with kudos concerning
her determined efforts to cleanse the world of
destitute black people,
brown people, poor people, and handicapped people
before they -
the black people, brown people, poor people, and
handicapped people ever had a chance to be seen,
to be heard, to become part of the "Better Society."
Vladimir, Genghis, Mao, Togo,
and the others are always astonished and amazed
at how Saint Sanger
achieved so much with only words
and a play upon human ignorance.
They acknowledged that she accomplished what they could
not with bayonets, bullets, and bombs.
And, they are equally touched by the fact
that Saint Sanger's philosophy continues to predominate.

CHESTER ALFONSO

44

Someone decided that
one month of living in the womb
was long enough to live.
Someone decided that
two months of living in the womb
was too long a life; therefore, that life had to end.
And, because one month and two months
of life was terminated,
those lives will
never have a birthday, sit in a baby's nursery,
or walk from a bedroom into a kitchen to grab a cookie.
Someone decided three months of life in the womb
would not remain in that womb for four months of life.
And, so, three months of life was wiped away.
This means the disposed life will
never taste a blueberry muffin,
or ride a surf board as it moves over Pacific Ocean waves.
Some live person decides that
four months of life in a woman's belly
does not deserve to emerge from that belly;

8^10 *(Eight to the Tenth Power)*

therefore,

that life will be executed for crimes not committed,

cut to pieces for thoughts not yet conjured,

destroyed before it can ever laugh.

Every hour, of every day, somewhere on the planet,

some conscientious human, living among us,

decides that

a life will be done away with,

will never hear or speak to a mother, father,

neighbor, teacher, minister, sister, brother, friend;

will never appreciate the flowers growing

in a nearby park or hear a puppy's bark.

All the time – all over the world –

someone or groups of someones

become God, become judge, become prosecutor,

become jury, become tribunal,

become the electric chair's switchman,

become the hanging noose's operator.

Every hour, in every corner of the planet,

someone takes on God-like power

and becomes the final arbitrator,

becomes the Grim Reaper,
becomes the slaughter house's supervisor,
becomes the firing squad.
Someone becomes the terminator,
the life-ender, the runier,
the iconoclast, the annihilator,
the demolisher, the killer.

45

In the Macy's dressing room,
she tried on new pairs of jeans;
turning to the left, back to the right,
looking over her shoulders,
hoping the new designs
would make her body appear slimmer,
more attractive
to the boys, the men who were bound to stare,
smile and act downright silly.
Perhaps they will acquire enough balls to
offer kind words, encouraging and inviting words,
which always cause any woman
to have a deliriously positive frame of mind.

8^10 *(Eight to the Tenth Power)*

Maybe her upstairs neighbor will

finally ask her out.

After months of worry, at last, she felt right.

It had been worth it.

The final act had taken place. And, she was happy.

It had been her decision, alone.

No one, other than the folks at the clinic, knew.

She tried-on a short, transparent blouse

that enhanced her prominent breasts.

Damn, right, it was the right choice.

Not even the guys she'd slept with knew.

They wouldn't have cared, anyway.

What losers.

She turned sideways.

She knew, for sure, she was as sexy as she'd ever been.

Next time she'll be more careful.

46

The ready-witted, lucent,

knowledgeable, intelligent class

say:

"There are already too many of

CHESTER ALFONSO

'Them,'

as it is.

We all know 'They' cannot be properly taken care of.

There's simply too many of

'Them'

wandering, hungry, without love, without protection."

The smart, ready-witted, lucent,

knowledgeable, intelligent class

say:

"What about the women addicted to crack cocaine?

The thirteen-year old girls and even the younger ones?

What do you do about the ones who

are raped by a disarranged, diseased

Rwandan or some illegal immigrant from Albania?

Or, what about the ones already

heading for the long prison

sentences?"

The smart, ready-witted, lucent,

knowledgeable, intelligent class

continually say

positive things about Thomas Robert Malthus

8^10 *(Eight to the Tenth Power)*

and similar herds of wise men.

Sometimes, they even praise

the Club of Rome and its Committee of 300.

47

Before He or She can feel a breeze

He or She is put to rest, extinguished, annihilated,

made invisible,

cut to pieces, removed bit-by-bit,

eliminated.

48

<u>Pause</u>

Old man Elmo

kept pondering, wondering, ruminating about

the great songwriters

and why they always wrote about war.

Always about the killings taking place on the battle fields

where young lives are lost, mangled,

wounded, scarred for eternity.

Left, many of them,

in private trenches of blood

and the loneliness of their personal pain and suffering.

CHESTER ALFONSO

Bodies too proud to ask for mercy

or seek any type understanding.

Defying till their last breath,

until their lonely, unceremonious permanent death.

The songwriters,

the ones who are brilliantly gifted

with the lyrics and the rhymes,

have always,

Elmo knew,

written about the terrible tragedy of conflict and battle,

how the human soul and the

unseen, deeply engraved human spirit

are laid to waste by others claiming to also be human.

The lyricist: European, African, South American,

Asian, Native American,

Latino, Australian Aborigine, North American;

they sit for hours, days, months, and years

penning words and music that sell in the

hundred of millions.

Words and music that make the young

take to the street to protest the killings

8^10 *(Eight to the Tenth Power)*

incurred by the latest stupid decisions
that caused the latest stupid war.
Their words, their themes
talk about how the USA President,
the British's Prime Minister, the President of France
and the crazed, power-hungry leaders of
other overly-developed nations,
send poor boys and poor girls off
to dastard lands to die for less than dastard causes.
Send them to kill other poor people who have
never harmed their overly-developed nation or them.
Rich nations sending their poor to kill those who are even
more poor.
Killing for the sake of killing,
for the sake of displaying moral superiority
espoused by the never-to-be-poor,
because the never-to-be-poor have the power
and the desire to promote the killing of the helpless.
And, the songs, and the words of the protest writers,
with their sad-looking singers and well-educated poets,
become louder and cover more territory than the howitzers,

than the exploding bombs.
Because, unlike the howitzers and the exploding bombs,
the songs and the poems are shrouded in
righteousness
and speak against superior nations invading, occupying
and destroying
less-superior nations.
The lyrics, the words provoke sentimental thought,
condemnation,
blame, denunciation, and shame.
Sometimes the listeners shed tears,
wring nervous hands, as they, the lyrics - the words,
skillfully and melodically put together,
make the listeners condemn, even more,
the taking of precious human life
by a stronger, more powerful force.
Elmo thinks that they – these songwriters – must be blind
if they cannot see the senseless killings,
every day,
taking place
on the same street where they

8^10 *(Eight to the Tenth Power)*

sit and compose their lyrics.

Taking place

in the apartment complexes and the houses next door.

Right in front of them.

Don't they know the lovers of their songs

continue to take innocent life

without giving that life a chance to

say hello or goodbye?

Don't they know the terminated life will never have a

chance to ever bob and weave

in appreciation of the lyrics these geniuses put to paper?

Is there a great writer,

film maker, a person of fame

willing and brave enough,

Elmo continually asks,

to tell the world, to shock the world

with tales of genocide against

the helpless

that sleeps in the womb?

49

Imagine

never touching your ear, not knowing if you have an ear.
Imagine never frowning because of an ill advised comment,
never finishing a novel, a television show, a recital.
Imagine never starring into a starless night.
Try placing yourself in the position of
imminent death without a chance to beg for salvation.
Try anticipating being cut to pieces – slowly,
by hands that once swore to save life.
Think how it would be to have a long spinal needle inject
deadly chemicals into your heart.
Imagine that.
Try justifying
eliminating millions upon millions with no excuse other
than:
"It is convenient. It is available.
It is mine; therefore, I can do whatever I please with 'It'."
Saying, very smartly:
"I believe in 'Choice.'"
Try justifying
sending unarmed, weak and voiceless
innocents

8^10 *(Eight to the Tenth Power)*

up against crude instruments of death

and the uncaring, selfless

"Hands of Annihilators."

Try rationalizing

the defense of peace, the protestation of war,

the end to hunger,

while with no remorse, supporting and justifying

the killing of those

who cannot defend themselves.

50

In the USA, alone, more'n a million a year.

Ain't that something?

Is that progress?

Is that, "Having it together?"

Is that, "Keepin' it real?"

How many are too many? How many is enough?

Would a hundred million be too many?

How about five-hundred million?

What's an acceptable figure?

51

There's this man;

CHESTER ALFONSO

weird sorta fellow,
going 'round saying there's been more of these killings,
called abortions,
in a single year
than all the killings done by all the wars,
starting with the American War of Independence,
back in 1775.
Tells everybody
to add the numbers and see what they come
up with.
Funny part:
These current victims that are being made dead,
ain't
ever carried any weapons.
They never went 'round beating anybody to death,
and they ain't ever shot at anybody with any type of
gun, slingshot or bow and arrow.
They didn't illegally cross anybody's border,
break any treaties,
or steal any secrets.
Still-all-n-all,

8^10 *(Eight to the Tenth Power)*

throughout this world,

'bout 45 million are

being slaughtered every year.

That comes to 'bout 123,287 a day.

That ain't counting the ones

nobody knows 'bout. Nobody reporting on.

Or, the RU-486 ones,

the Mifepristone ones,

and the Methotrexate ones.

All that dying

and not a single gravestone bearing

the name of any of the victims.

This man said

you can stroll through Cimetière du Père-LaChaise,

Arlington, Somme, Oise-Aisne,

Corozal, Myles Standish, Arnhem Oosterbeek, Rhone,

Cimetière Notre-Dame-des-Neiges, Forest

Lawn, Woodland, Bayreuth Friedhof, Weissensee,

Tikhvin, Novodevichy, Cimetière de Passy,

Hamilton Road, Bath Abbey, Wolvercote,

and all the other graveyards in

Asia, Africa, Australia, South America, and North America
and you will not find a plaque, a gravesite,
not even a simple marker.
There will be no signs with names,
dates of birth, dates of death,
or reasons explaining their death.
Look all you want, he said,
and you'll never find, for these victims, anything like the
"Tomb of the Unknown Soldier,"
so many countries use to honor
the death of their unidentified soldiers.
No, there is nothing commemorating these
unidentified deaths.

52

Don't expect
a crime scene investigation.
Don't expect to see groups of reporters shoving each
other for better positioning.
Don't expect to hear a mayor giving up-to-minute updates,
or witness a gathering of curious neighbors
asking for the victims' names.

8^10 *(Eight to the Tenth Power)*

Don't expect to observe

a grieving household filled

with sympathy cards and flowers.

Ain't gonna have no New Orleans jazz band leading

or following a funeral procession.

The Thunderbirds or the Blue Angels

will not perform a fly-over.

No preacher will give last rites as he stands

over a closed casket.

Don't' expect

to see their names in the obituary section of any

newspaper.

You will not attend a class where sociology professors

will spend time explaining

why millions each year,

and more'n a hundred thousand each day are destroyed.

Don't expect

a slow moving hearse – with a body inside –

going to a two-hundred-year-old cemetery,

or questions about why God saw fit to take such a

young and precious life.

Don't expect anything.

53

In betwixt, somewhere and somehow,

in between

infinitesimal and insignificant,

they

are the *Inconspicuous,*

the *Inconsequential,*

the *Inconvenient,*

the *Invisible,*

and *Indecorous*

waiting to be added to the piles

of the *Undesired,*

the *Unwelcomed,*

the *Unaccountable,*

the *Unbecoming,*

and the *Unwanted.*

They are no different than the 13 million the
"progressive" people of China add each year to their pile.
Or, the annual two or three million thrown onto the stack
by the lads of the new capitalists' cities of Russia:

8^10 *(Eight to the Tenth Power)*

Moscow and Saint Petersburg;
while hip New Yorkers and debt ridden Californians,
not wanting to be outdone,
contribute their share with almost a million each year.
See those lines, down the street, around the corner?
Those are teenagers, first time lovers,
old ladies, sanctified women.
Some are married. Some never gonna be.
In the lines are
women standing and waiting for God-only-knows
what ugly occurrence that might soon
be visited upon their bodies.
Men: boyfriends, women-users, rape artists,
high-flung lawyers, stock brokers, construction workers,
star athletes, and unemployed hanger-ons are
nowhere to be seen.
Could be they are already off to addresses down the road
preparing to send another fetus to the
knife, the suction cup, the needle.
To a place in the line.

54

But what about those who are too young?
And, the ones who've been raped?
And those forced into prostitution?
If the rape victim, the prostitute becomes impregnated,
would they be spared by Jehovah if they
were to destroy the life they carry?
Are they not worthy of salvation?
Should they be lumped with the ones
who opted for the procedure because of their vainness?
Will the poor children, mauled and made pregnant by old
men, be lumped by Jehovah, with those
who aborted because giving life would
be too inconvenient, too bothersome, too troublesome?
And, what of those made pregnant
by their fathers, their brothers, their uncles,
or by mad men threatening to leave them beaten, dead by
the side of a rural road?
Those pitiful souls, choosing abortion,
should be forgiven, don't you think?
God, don't you think, will look down
upon them with mercy?

8^10 *(Eight to the Tenth Power)*

And, that will be good,

don't you think?

55

The elected leader,

more popular than anyone might

have imagined,

stood on the floor of the U.S. Senate.

His hair having been perfectly styled,

spoke eloquently, seriously,

and with a steel purpose regarding

the right of women to make their own choices

concerning their lives and bodies;

whether these choices involve

attending law school,

being a stay-at-home mom,

or to terminate a pregnancy.

It, he so forcefully told the other senators,

was every woman's individual right.

Those who said otherwise were living in the dark ages.

Were attempting to dictate to women how they should

control their bodies.

And, nothing, he said, speaks to that control
more so than controlling
a woman's most basic right:
whether or not to reproduce.
The senator and his lovely wife,
a professor at a Washington, D.C. university,
had three children, all boys:
thirteen, fifteen, and eighteen-years-old.
The family home, while in Washington, D.C.,
was a four bedroom structure, in Georgetown.
Whenever possible they attended
the Georgetown Presbyterian Church.
They always said their prayers;
asking for forgiveness and blessings
for all mankind, particularly for the less fortunate.
Sometimes, late at night, while the senator snored,
the professor thought how much she had wanted a
daughter.
That is why they had tried pregnancy for the third time.
But, with God's blessings,
they had conceived another boy, Ricky,

8^10 *(Eight to the Tenth Power)*

who turned out to be brilliant, extremely
smart and fun to be around.
Her children – indeed, her entire family, was her life
She could not fathom an existence without any of them.
But, however, no matter how she tries not to,
she always remembers the train ride
from New Haven to Montreal.
It had been her sophomore year of college.
The affair with a local, older musician
was an experimental endeavor.
She had wanted to know what it would be like
to have a relationship with the mature and popular
man, who was not white.
He had taught her so much.
He knew more about math, science, politics and philosophy
than she would ever know.
Then, as she had been warned by friends,
she became pregnant with the black musician's child.
Everyone, at this private, all-girl's university,
knew the routine:
Telephone the clinic in Montreal.

Make an appointment.

Arrange transportation.

Be prepared to pay nearly two thousand American dollars.

Stay three days and return to campus.

Act as if nothing had happened.

She could still see him at the piano.

She could still be moved by memories of his shy laughter.

Could still hear the revolutionary

rhetoric and the tender, poetic words

he always spoke while making love.

Next week the senator will address a forum of women

at the Four Seasons Hotel, in Philadelphia.

Again, his message will center on the

conservatives' evil battle against

Planned Parenthood.

No matter what the conservatives said,

he knew he had to stay focused on the organization's

overall health assistance programs.

Regardless of the baiting, he would not slip into the

abortion arena;

even though he knew, because the Planned Parenthood

8^10 *(Eight to the Tenth Power)*

leadership had told him
that terminating pregnancies was
their number one priority;
especially, if the mother happened to be black or brown.
But, he and his wife were liberals,
and black and brown
people loved liberals.
Didn't matter whether their future black and brown
children were executed,
massacred, and butchered before being born,
they still worshipped
and believed
every word spoken by liberals.

56

Pamela Daniels and Todd White graduated the same year
from the same high school in Chester, Virginia.
Then, together, they attended the Chester campus of
John Tyler Community College.
After one year they both dropped out of John Tyler.
Pamela became a stocker at Kohl's, on Route 10.
Todd, unable to find work, joined the U.S. Army.

CHESTER ALFONSO

His Armed Services Vocational Aptitude Battery
scores qualified him for
any U.S. Army Military Occupational Specialty.
He chose: *Food Service Specialist. Cook.
92G: Ninety-Two-Golf*
because the technical center for Ninety-Two-Golf
is at Fort Lee, Virginia;
only a few miles from Chester,
where Pamela and he had grown up.
He graduating from his technical school
with honors.
On September 25,
a very warm and beautiful day in Chesterfield County,
Pamela and Todd were married.
Two weeks later they were separated:
Todd was being assigned to Fort Riley, Kansas.
Pamela decided to remain in Chester.
They agreed that after he got settled,
out in Junction City,
he was going to send for Pamela.
In December, Kohl's gave Pamela a pay raise.

8^10 *(Eight to the Tenth Power)*

On a cold and wintery Kansas day,

the 1st Infantry Division – "Big Red One,"

was notified that it had to deploy

to Afghanistan.

Todd didn't even have enough

time to come back to Chester to

kiss, hug and make love with Pamela.

His food service supervisor told him to suck it up.

Be a soldier. Be a man.

Told Private First Class Todd Daniels,

everybody was leaving somebody they loved.

It was only gonna be for six months.

But, once in Afghanistan,

the six month deployment stretched into twelve months.

Back stateside the spouses left behind

at Fort Riley, in Junction City and in Manhattan, Kansas

received great support from

the Fort Riley, at-large, military community.

The only folks supporting Pamela, back in Chester,

Virginia, were her coworkers at Kohl's.

Her staunchest supporter was Wayne Thomas,

her pot-bellied, beer-smelling supervisor.
During late night stockings
and rearrangements of displays,
Wayne, whenever he had the chance,
would make comments about how pretty Pamela was.
How she must be very lonely.
How he would like to spend
a few private moments with her.
Two weeks after she had received Todd's email
telling her the deployment had
been extended by six months,
feeling emotionally empty, she decided
to have a beer with Wayne Thomas.
One beer led to several beers
and a long discussion about sex.
This led to her sleeping with her
pot-bellied, beer-smelling supervisor.
Pamela, a short time later, found out she was pregnant.
Then she received another email:
Todd telling her he had been selected
the Big Red One's "Soldier of the Quarter,"

8^10 *(Eight to the Tenth Power)*

gotten promoted to corporal and was

sending her a special present.

Three weeks later, at a

Planned Parenthood Center,

in Richmond, Virginia,

Pamela Daniels had her first abortion.

She never returned to Kohl's.

She never again spoke to Wayne Thomas.

57

The bewitching words of the old woman

spoke about things no one could comprehend,

not to mention, believe.

And the numbers and words she wrote on the paper:

"Eight to the tenth power,

which is

One billion, 73 million, 741 thousand, eight hundred and

twenty-four.

8^10 = 1,073,741, 824.

And, the number keeps rising."

58

CHESTER ALFONSO

And,

these, the aborted ones,

who

could have,

should have,

would have,

been introduced to life,

this year,

were it not for a privileged group of Choosers:

1 million who might have had freckles.

1 million who might have been named "John."

1 million potential doctors.

3 million who might have had brown eyes.

1 million who might have become police, firefighters.

4 million possible schoolteachers.

2 million who might have been named "Tom."

4 million who might have had blue eyes.

5 million possible construction workers.

1 million who might have been named "Mary."

2 million possible elite, world-class athletes.

3 million who might have become soldiers.

8^10 *(Eight to the Tenth Power)*

1 million who might have had the opportunity to
be a great, loving, and protective husband, father.
1 million who might have become writers.
1 million possible ballerinas.
2 million who might have had the name "Katrina."
2 million who might have become great chefs.
1 million who might have loved watching baseball.
3 million with the possibility of becoming mothers.
1 million who might have cared for the sick, the elderly.
1 million who might have been given the name "Michael."
and
4 million who might have regularly attended church.

59

East and west she plods along Central Avenue.
Between her pleas for small donations,
which are
ignored by everyone but a few tolerant tourists,
she continuously repeats:
"Where is my Lilly?"
The Albuquerque police have grown accustom to her
madness, sadness and despicable appearances.

CHESTER ALFONSO

They know enough about her to know she is of no danger
    to the citizens of their proud and peaceful city.
        They also know she was once a
    University of New Mexico graduate student,
        majoring in biological physics.
    That she came to the university by way of
        Decatur, Alabama.
    For whatever reason, one day she decided
        to stop attending classes.
She soon became a recluse and then a street person.
The clothes she wears are lifted from garbage bins.
    Regardless how hot the weather,
        she always wear several layers
of coats and dresses, with long pants underneath.
Her body, so filthy, has cease to give off an odor.
    The foods she eat are from the street or are
        discarded remnants
from cafes, restaurants, and bags of left-over's from some
        person's lunch.
    Those who had known her, during her student years,
        claims she was a most attractive woman.

8^10 *(Eight to the Tenth Power)*

Said she was absolutely brilliant.
Her mastering of both biology and physics was superior.
Her former professors still give her the highest praise.
Then it all ended. Something within her snapped.
Now from one end of Central Avenue to the other,
more than seventeen miles,
summer, fall, winter and spring -
she walks,
wrapped, she is, in her bundle of clothing.
Always murmuring:
"Where is my Lilly?"
The city takes her, ever so often,
to the county and state hospitals to be physically and
mentally examined.
Each time she is released only to be found
going from east to west and west to east
along the Avenue.
Then, one summer day,
engaged in conversation with her favorite person,
Policewoman Carmen Solo,
she said a few words more.

She said:

"That boy from across the street,

up north in Grand Rapids,

that boy never did write me that letter.

Never did tell me, after I headed back Down Home,

that he still loved me.

Carmen, that wasn't right.

Then, they took away what he had given me:

They took my Lilly."

Finally, looking lost,

she rose from the bus-stop bench,

smiled at Policewoman Solo,

and continued her walk down Central Avenue,

asking:

"Where is my Lilly?"

60

Lyesya was extremely nervous and totally afraid.

Maybe, she thought, this was a mistake.

She had lied to her faithful and strong husband, Jakob,

telling him she would be attending

a four day conference, in Warsaw, for her company.

8^10 *(Eight to the Tenth Power)*

Jakob expressed pride.

Said he would make sure their three children

were well taken care of.

Rather than Warsaw, however, Lyesya

was in a rundown house in Pruszkow, which was nearby.

The old house had very little, if any, heat.

The doctor – Jobal, was in the next room preparing.

Soon the procedure began.

Jobal gave her two aspirin.

Said he had no anesthesia.

Lyesya felt a pain greater than even the pain of giving birth.

Very quickly her entire life appeared before her eyes.

She heard a rumbling, a thunder like sound.

Then, seeping into her consciousness was

Bach's *"Sleepers Awake."*

She saw her favorite school teacher smiling at her

and her friend, Maggi, waving her hands.

A slight breeze entered the room,

reminding her of serenity,

of restfulness and tranquility.

The slight breeze swept over her naked body.

She thought she heard Jobal scream:

"Coś jest nie tak! Coś złego działo się, nie mogę powstrzymać bleedig.! "

("Something is wrong! Something bad has happened! I can't stop the bleeding.!)

Lyesya saw her children's faces. She saw Jakob.

She saw her father and her mother.

She saw nothing else.

Ever.

61

The Rio Muni girl, sitting outside a small café, in Bata, bent forward and rested her arms on her thighs.

Her face as black and smooth as Equatorial Guinea's newly discovered oil.

Her smile attempted to wash away whatever sins she had recently committed.

Her eyes: green and large and bright.

She could see everything.

She drank her Perrier water straight from the bottle.

With her tongue, she kept caressing her mid-sized lips.

She said she felt no guilt.

8^10 *(Eight to the Tenth Power)*

She set straight and pointed a manicured finger at a large,
well-dressed woman: Her mother.
Then, she waved.
She said the abortion laws of Equatorial Guinea
were fuzzy for some
but not for women like her:
Sexy, sophisticated, beautiful
and able to speak many languages.
To keep her mother, brothers and sisters happy,
and
to continually make her husband or keeper satisfied,
she would do whatever needed doing.
If that meant having a hundred abortions,
then she would have a hundred abortions.
This is Equatorial Guinea. This is not Japan.
Or, Norway. Or, America.
This is Bata.
This ain't no Hollywood or Paris.
She touched his hand. Held it. Look into his eyes.
She could see everything.
Maybe even his thoughts

and his forgotten, not yet occurred mistakes.

But, she said,

if he made her stomach swell,

she would not abort his child.

Said she would happily bring

his baby into the terrible world.

She bent her head low, kissed the hand she was holding.

Took his middle finger and sucked it like she was sucking

his most sensitive and in-need-of-sucking penis.

She looked up and asked if he would

like to take her

to her mother's house

or, perhaps, to his room in the overly expensive

Sofitel Malabo President Palace

and do crazy, wild and thrilling things with her body?

If he would like to spend more time

listening to her, teasing her?

If he would like to know the many pleasures

a Rio Muni girl is capable of providing a handsome man?

He said nothing.

She said her husband had spies.

8^10 *(Eight to the Tenth Power)*

They watch everything she does.

They were watching her, now.

But, it did not matter.

Her husband would enjoy her

description of what happened between them.

It would arouse him.

Make him, for a few minutes, more sexually capable.

She kept smiling.

Finally, she release his hand.

Then, she asked:

"Do you think God frowns on abortions?

Do you think He will forgive me?

Do you think, because I come from

the beaches of Rio Muni,

come from the very poor country of Equatorial Guinea,

God will ignore this sin called abortion?

Or, do you think I'll end up in the fire down below?"

62

It had been five years.

They, the years, had gone too fast.

He was now sixty-one.

CHESTER ALFONSO

His hair had thinned.
What was left, had changed colors.
His former mistress,
the one he had taken to that goddamned
Planned Parenthood shindig,
was now married to
some po-ass high school basketball coach.
But, it didn't matter.
He had finally become a very powerful man.
He had recently presided over the
openings of three new
Planned Parenthood Reproductive Service Clinics:
his sixteenth, seventeenth, and eighteenth.
The money, not from his ministry,
but from the good folks at Planned Parenthood,
was coming in faster than he could spend it.
And, with all the money he was receiving,
he had purchased a new Porsche and
a big house in the city's most restrictive community.
In his bedroom,
with three, huge, high-definition televisions,

8^10 *(Eight to the Tenth Power)*

all programmed and loaded with pornographic movies,
he was always entertaining
willing female souls anxious to relinquish
their morals and bodies in the name of
well prepared food, free drink and good cocaine.
He tried to recall just how many
women and young girls he had had sex with,
and how many he had made pregnant.
And, yes, each of the pregnant ones,
he had force to have an abortion.
At the ripe-old-age of sixty-one
he was still able to impregnate.
Poor, down-and-out black, brown, and white girls
continued to ride, with pride, in his new Porsche
and his older Mercedes.
The scum bitches were thrilled at being driven to
his massive, elaborately furnished,
gated-community house.
And, they always, while watching porn
on his three high-definition televisions,
did whatever he wanted them to do.

He never used a prophylactic.

And, they, these ignorant beauties,

almost never took any precautions against pregnancy.

Scary thought after scary thought rambled though his mind.

But, what the heck, he was a PhD from Yale.

This meant he was smarter than anyone else he knew.

Plus, he was a big-wheel in the abortion industry.

Well, not really "abortion industry,"

more like the "sanitation industry."

He and Planned Parenthood were protecting

America from the misfit, trifling, unworthy, dirty

future inhabitants threatening this great country.

Others may call it abortion;

we, at Planned Parenthood, he thought, call it sanitation.

63

Isadora Catalina de la Balc

walked across the lobby –

all eyes watching her suggestive stride.

She took the stairs to the third floor.

The rain had made her pensive, reflective, melancholy.

The interior decorators had done her office well.

8^10 *(Eight to the Tenth Power)*

Perusing the weekly international human rights report,
she immediately saw the ugliness
taking place near Rumbek, South Sudan.
Second Jesus Wayya, the stupid Dinka Agar revolutionary,
and his Christian terrorist group, Second Rising,
had gone on a holy war rampage.
In two days they
had slaughtered more than ninety Muslims,
many of them women and children.
The report cited one of Wayya's
silly and childish statements:
*"The only thing the dregs of mankind deserve
are to be buried in the bowels of the earth.
We, the Second Rising, will kill and kill until
every single believer in the false god Muhammad is
slain and sent to the hellhole they and their offspring
are destined to be."*
Isadora Catalina de la Balc,
a mestizo from the Vitacura neighborhood
of Santiago, Chili;
a graduate of the

Pontificia Universidad Católica de Chile's School of Law, and later a holder of a doctorate in International Economics from Princeton University, looked from her window and saw the parts of Geneva she always found cold and impersonal. It had been a tiring and intriguing, but sensational life. After being pampered by Santiago's rich and famous, she was flown to New York City and motored to Princeton, New Jersey. Nearly five years of intense study and then the PhD. Prior to leaving Princeton with her PhD in hand, Isadora was recruited by the United Nations. At the United Nations she worked in the office of Human Rights and Human Development. After two years she was offered a most prestigious U.N. position in Geneva: Head of the United Nations Human Settlement Program. Along the way she had made several sacrifices. Some were worthy and good. Others were unworthy and bad. She was well aware of her major problem: Sex.

8^10 *(Eight to the Tenth Power)*

And, because she could never be totally sexually satisfied,
three times she had allowed herself to become pregnant.
Each time weighing the consequences,
she had made the decision to destroy the fetus.
In New York City, as opposed to Chili,
getting an abortion was inexpensive and easy.
Now, she believed she was again pregnant.
This time bearing the fruit
of some damned, computer technician.
Some lowly paid machine mechanic assigned to make sure
her department's computers
were always in perfect condition.
He was the only man she had slept with during the
previous six months.
My God, she thought, his income was half her's.
He did not speak Spanish, German, or French.
Did not like the opera. He dressed like shit.
He was not aware of any topic
other than his damned computers
and the weight-lifting equipment at
Geneva's Holmes Place Fitness.

Yet, as a dare to herself,
she had allowed him to make love to her.
She had to admit, he was sensational in bed.
So, it continued. At least four times a week.
Neither of them could get enough of each other,
sexually, that is.
The only reason he had gotten the job in Geneva
was because the people in the Brussels' office,
where he formerly performed his
"information systems" magic,
were tired of his
one-dimensional behavior.
She picked up the report and started towards the
conference room.
This evening, when he stopped by for his
regular dose of grunts and groans,
she would tell him she was carrying his child.
This would be the first lover she would have ever told
about being pregnant.
She would not mention any of her previous abortions.
Despite his dullness and lack of sophistication,

8^10 *(Eight to the Tenth Power)*

he was basically a good man.

However, she, again, noted,

as she walked into the conference room and

took her seat at the head of the long table,

he was not good enough to meet her family,

back in Santiago.

Therefore, this pregnancy, like the others,

would be terminated.

64

The smaller house in Croydon had been replaced

by a larger one in Edinburg.

This is where the girls,

having completed their medical studies,

were now in residence at

the Western General Hospital and the

Longmore House Hospital.

Najib Ahmed Shakir no longer prayed each day.

He had become almost completely Westernized.

His wife and daughters the same.

They had started studying to be, of all things, Lutherans.

Allah, the Quar'an and the ways of Islam

were no longer important parts of their lives.
He, his wife, Sandra and their daughters
were doing their best to
purge their memories of all Islamic thought.
They realized the dangers accompanying
such a religious transformation
from Islam to any other religion but it did not matter.
Save for his profession, he had become a new man.
In addition to the bigger home in Edinburgh,
he now drove a 7-Series BMW automobile.
His wife a Jaguar XK.
His medical practice, terminating life, had grown.
He had more women anxious for abortions
than he could have ever imagined.
It seemed as if the new craze was to become pregnant
and then rush forward for the removal of the fetus.
Because of this, he encouraged his older daughter to assist.
Then, the other two started rendering their services.
At the end of his fourth year in Edinburgh,
based on his wife's precise recordkeeping,
they were performing more than

8^10 *(Eight to the Tenth Power)*

three thousand abortions each year.

He was, finally, a happy man.

65

The apartment on Zidovska steza, in Ljubljana,
is always warm, bright, and filled with playfulness.
They had motored from Hamburg to Hanover.
From there they took a bus
to a village near the Frankfurt International Airport.
After spending three days in a tiny hotel in Moerfelden,
they boarded a train from Frankfurt to Munich.
From there they took another train
to Ljubljana, Slovenia.
This is where they have lived for the past four years.
He makes his living repairing any housing items
or automobiles in need of repair.
He is referred to as: Frank the Handyman.
She works at a day care center minding
small children.
Frank Vill and Mildred Jessup make a lovely couple,
this is what everyone says.
He loves to work with his hands,

while she uses her carefully arranged emotions to
provide comfort to small, growing children.
Neither Frank nor Mildred
mentions what took place in Hamburg.
They never talk about their past.
They never discuss the possibilities of
Mildred giving birth.
On Sunday mornings they attend a small Christian church.
There, they issue their weekly prayers.
Then, regardless the weather, they walk, holding hands,
through Tivoli Park.
Seldom do they speak to each other.
They do, however, smile at people who pass by.
Back at their apartment, on Zidovska steza,
Mildred always prepares a nice potato soup.
Then, they listen to music, usually jazz.
When the sounds of a muted trumpet or a tenor saxophone,
or whatever, fades into oblivion,
they undress and silently make love.

66

On the island of Sylt,

8^10 *(Eight to the Tenth Power)*

between Germany and Denmark,

Herr Bauer

drinks his warm Dallmayr Prodomo.

Twitching his nose towards the freezing waters,

he listens to the sounds he has been hearing

for the past eight years.

They are a mixture of pain, cries for help,

laughter, warning, instruction, and prayer.

The sounds have nearly driven him mad.

There is no other person he can talk to about this.

So, each evening, drinking his coffee,

he readies himself by standing very still

near the water's edge.

Standing, silently, with no muscle movement,

save the twitching of his nose, he listens.

Last night he though he could hear voices asking:

"Kennen Sie schon unsere Mütter gesehen?"

"Kennen Sie schon unsere Mütter gesehen?"

("Have you seen our mothers?")

("Have you seen our mothers?")

All night long the voices

continued to ask the same question.
Then several weeks prior, he thought the sounds were
whispering some other song.
For three entire days all he could hear,
coming from the waters, were:
"Heute ist ein Kind auf der Erde geboren.
Heute ist ein Kind auf der Erde geboren.
Heute ist die Herrlichkeit Gottes scheint überall
Für alle der Welt."
("Today a child is born on earth.
Today a child is born on earth.
Today the glory of God shines everywhere
For all of the world.")

67

Though a believer and devotee of The Buddha,
the Sage of Chugu-ji,
having read and understood all religious thought,
often immerses himself in the words
expressed in the Christian Bible.
During moments when he allows himself to become
as silent as the shy breeze and

8^10 *(Eight to the Tenth Power)*

as peaceful as an unspoken trust,
he will, to himself, recite the words
reflected so eloquently in the
Book of Genesis:
*"So God created man in his own image,
in the image of God created he him;
male and female created he them.
And God blessed them, and God
said unto them, Be fruitful, and multiply,
and replenish the earth and subdue it:
and have dominion over the fish of the sea,
and over the fowl of the air, and over every living thing that
moveth upon the earth."*
Afterwards, the Sage of Chugu-ji's
thoughts most often move to the words of
his master, The Buddha:
*"Whoever offends an innocent, pure and faultless person,
the evil (of his act) rebounds on that fool, even as fine dust
thrown against the wind."*
Then, lowering his head, the Sage of Chugu-ji, weeps.

68

CHESTER ALFONSO

Fifty/ maybe 100/ 200/ maybe, even a billion.

Is there anybody counting?

Who cares? Who gives a damn?

8^10 *(Eight to the Tenth Power)*

But keep your eyes below us, for coming near
Is the river of blood – in which boils everyone
Whose violence hurt others.
"The Inferno of Dante"
- Dante Alighieri

Chester Alfonso – a pseudonym - was born and raised in Selma, Alabama. He is a graduate of Auburn University, Montgomery, Alabama. He attended graduate school at Auburn and the University of Melbourne, Melbourne, Victoria, Australia. He and his wife currently reside in Virginia.

www.ingramcontent.com/pod-product-compliance
Lightning Source LLC
Chambersburg PA
CBHW071419160426
43195CB00013B/1745